HUDDERSFIELD
MEMORIES

The publishers would like to thank the following companies for their

support in the production of this book

Main Sponsor

K D Decoratives Ltd

Armitage Sykes LLP Solicitors

J&E Dickenson, Longley Farm

Drakes Bar Furniture

Dresser Roots

W Fisher & Sons (Tilers) Ltd

Holset Turbochargers

W T Johnson

Merrie England Coffee Shops Ltd

Myers Group

J B Schofield & Sons Ltd

Shaw & Hallas

Swift Blinds

Syngenta

Taylor & Lodge

Trojan Plastics Limited

Quarmby Promotions Ltd

Queensgate Market Tenant's Association

Wood Auto Supplies Ltd

First published in Great Britain by True North Books Limited
England HX3 6AE
01422 344344

ISBN 1 903204 86 0

Text, design and origination by True North Books Limited
Printed and bound by The Amadeus Press Limited

HUDDERSFIELD MEMORIES

Contents

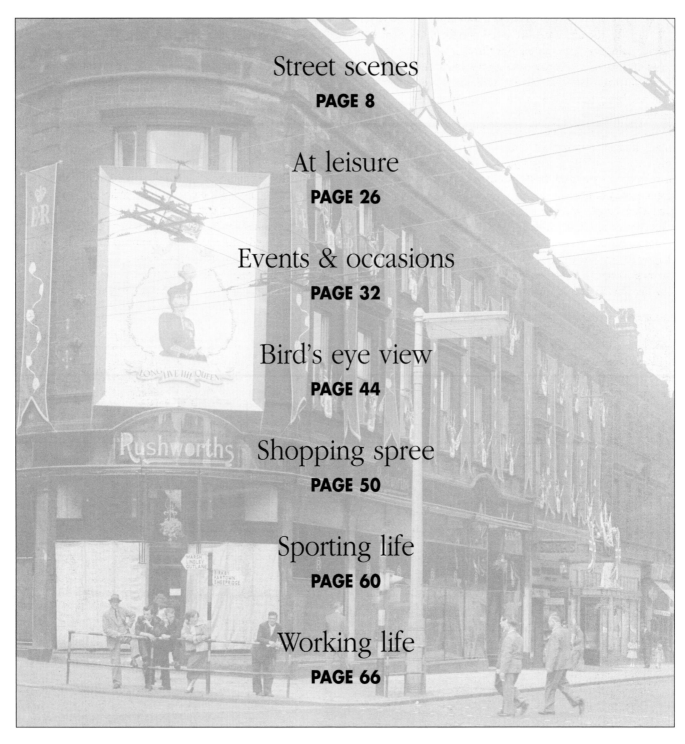

Introduction

Memories gain a rosy hue as the years roll by. We fondly recall the days of our youth and long for the times that we loved to return. They never can. The generations through which we have lived and the ones our parents experienced seem lost forever. Until, that is, we have the chance to use something that will bring them back to life. Thanks to the magic of the camera we can resurrect the precious past and 'Huddersfield Memories' does just that. This delightful book, containing so many images from the last century, does more than jog the memory as, with its glorious photographs and poignant captions, you are taken back to a time when a calmer, less frenetic way of life was to be found in our town. Relive the age when people window-shopped on Buxton Road or sat and chatted about the world at large. Peek into the department stores of days gone by and bring back to mind the happy frolics in the parks. Mixed in there is heartache and sadness. They are part of our heritage as well. The days that the heavens rained fire and destruction upon us are painfully remembered. Younger readers can see for themselves what it meant to have a home reduced to rubble, though the town was luckier than most in that the Luftwaffe was more interested in the industry in larger conurbations such as Sheffield and Leeds than our neck of the woods. But let those youngsters also appreciate the kindred spirit of the war years as communities pulled together to console one another and build a brighter future. As you turn the pages let the mood of nostalgia fill your thoughts and allow you to wallow in those days of yesteryear. The book makes no apologies for asking you to say, 'In my day it was ...,' because these pages will prove just how accurate the memory is, or not, as the case may be. When you take this journey through time you need no Tardis. All that is needed is a personal history and an interest in having those brain cells stimulated. Prepare to take a journey to the days of humbugs and gobstoppers. Get dressed in floor length skirts or minis and kinky boots. Don a flat cap and a pair of overalls as you get ready to roll back the years.

However, Huddersfield is more than just woollens and worsted, mill chimneys and 'ee by gum'. It has a proud history that helps it stand as a major player in Yorkshire's heritage and, of course, is one of the last outposts of the White Rose territory before the land gives way to our arch rivals on the other side of the Pennines in Lancashire. There is evidence that the Romans settled at Cambodunum, above Outlane, on the road they built from Manchester to Tadcaster. An altar was discovered in the 18th century and later discoveries of heating chambers and traces of Roman buildings strongly suggest that a garrison was based at Slack. After the Romans withdrew in the 5th century, marauding Picts and Scots took their toll on the area and it was not until Saxon times that some element of stability was established. Places such as Meltham, Deighton, Honley and Almondbury owe their origins to this era, with the latter being particularly important as Paulinus, the first Bishop of York, built a church there, dedicated to St Alban. However, serenity was short lived as the Vikings turned their attention to our shores. Netherthong, Fixby, Linthwaite and Slaithwaite are just a few of the examples of place names of Danish origin.

It was after the Norman Conquest that official mention of Huddersfield as an entity was first made. The Domesday Book, the record of the national survey ordered by William the Conqueror, makes reference to 'Odersfelt' and it is not too much of a leap from that spelling to the modern name of our town. 'Huddersfield' loosely translates as 'Huthere's field' or 'Hather's field', from the name of the person who once owned the land at the heart of the settlement. In c1130 William the Conqueror's grandson, King Stephen, built a fortification on Castle Hill and later passed on the guardianship of the castle to Henri de Laci. By 1272 the de Laci family was granted the privilege of holding a weekly market in Almondbury, but the district achieved a certain notoriety in 1307 when a man was murdered in the castle and his body thrown from the ramparts for animals to devour. The castle was demolished not long after this dark deed was perpetrated.

Huddersfield gradually grew during the centuries that followed, but did not truly gain prominence until the days of the industrial revolution. From being a large village in the 18th century, one of several that had a domestic weaving industry, its importance burgeoned and benefited from construction of the Calder and Marsden canals. Standedge Tunnel, opened in 1811, linked the

Huddersfield Narrow Canal through to Ashton under Lyne and was feted as a marvel of modern engineering, being the longest, highest and deepest canal tunnel in Britain. The locality's traditional textile industry, together with coal and water supplies, stimulated ancillary dyestuff, chemical and heavy-engineering industries. By the early 19th century, a plethora of mills covered the landscape, but also brought unrest in the form of the Luddite insurrection. The Luddites were members of organised bands of craftsmen who rioted for the destruction of the textile machinery that was displacing them. The movement began in the vicinity of Nottingham towards the end of 1811 and in the next year spread to Yorkshire, Lancashire, Derbyshire, and Leicestershire. The activists were generally masked and operated at night. Their leader, real or imaginary, was known as King Ludd, after a probably mythical Ned Ludd. They eschewed violence against persons and often enjoyed local support. However, in 1812 a band of Luddites was shot down under the orders of a threatened Marsden employer named William Horsfall. He was afterward murdered in reprisal and three of his killers were executed after a fourth turned King's evidence against them to save his own neck. The modern face of our town was established in Victorian times and many of its architectural marvels date from this time. It was granted county borough status in 1868.

But it is to the last century that we now turn for our look at 'Huddersfield Memories', the latest in the series of True North books about the town and district that are the birthplace of many famous sons. The major part of cricketer Wilfrid Rhodes' career took place in the early 20th century and GD Harrison, the designer of many American cathedral organs, began his days in Huddersfield. Actors James Mason, Patrick Stewart and Gorden Kaye, the entertainer Roy Castle and Baron Wilson of Rievaulx, the former prime minister, J Harold Wilson, all have roots here. So, now prepare for a dip into yesteryear that will make you long for days that can never be revisited in the flesh, though this is a good second best. Reach for a glass of dandelion and burdock, filled from a stone jar, and pick up a penny Arrow bar to chew on. Light up a Craven A, 'for your throat's sake', Wind up the gramophone, put a new needle into the stylus and let Nat 'King' Cole soothe you with 'Mona Lisa' as you wallow in nostalgia.

Street scenes

This photograph could almost be entitled 'Transport through the ages'. There are people using Shanks's pony as they amble across St George's Square, motorcars, a horse and cart, an old Scammel wagon, a tram and trolley buses. The square is crisscrossed by the power lines needed to provide the juice for Huddersfield's public transport. The cabling first appeared at the start of the last century when electrification of the old steam tram routes was completed. By the summer of 1902, the fleet of electric trams numbered 61. They were all of the open topped variety. So public transport was a cold, chilly and damp experience for our Edwardian forebears. The paying passengers soon made their displeasure clear and tops were fitted before too many years had passed. This photograph was taken in 1938 when tramcars had nearly run their full course. They were gradually phased out in favour of the trolley-buses and the last car ran on the Brighouse route on 29 June 1940. The Belisha beacon outside the George Hotel was named for the Minister of Transport of the mid 1930s, Leslie Hore-Belisha, who had been responsible for overseeing the introduction of many road safety measures, including driving tests, urban speed limits and Percy Shaw's cats' eyes. By the time of this scene Hore-Belisha was installed as Minister for War as we prepared for the inevitable clash with Hitler.

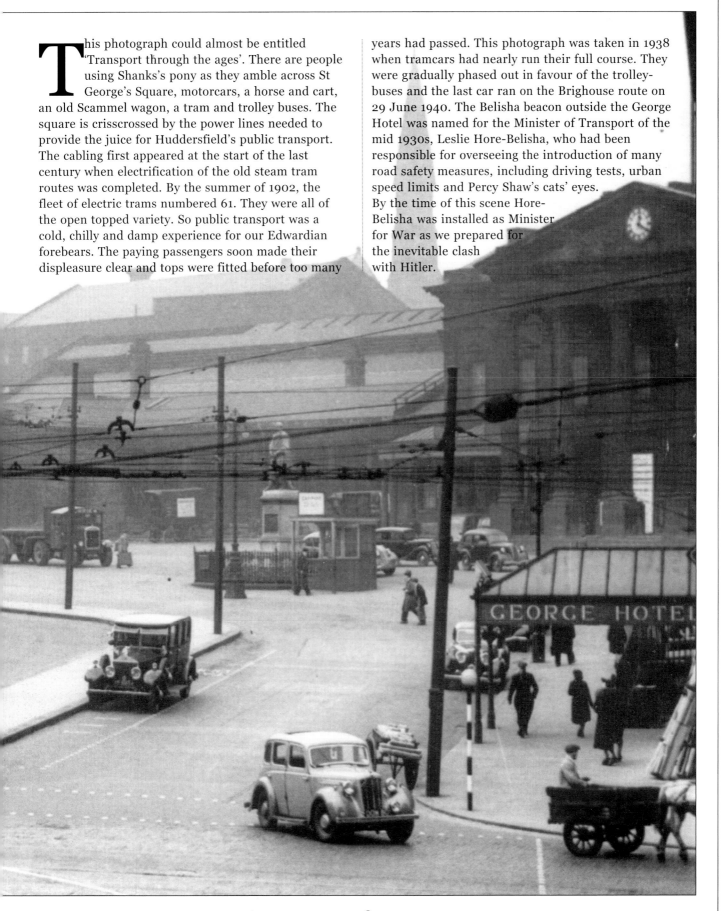

Right: Some of us took our lives in our own hands when getting on or off buses before they were fitted with driver operated doors. The open platform was an invitation to a passenger to hop on board as the vehicle slowed to take a corner. Other intrepid souls could not wait until the appropriate bus stop and baled out quite happily at any speed up to about 15 mph. There were occasions when it seemed that conductors played games with their public. Most of them possessed a warped sense of humour, or so it seemed to those of us who were on the last minute. How often did we run towards the bus stop, have the conductor look us straight in the eye, watch him estimate our distance from the platform and then see him ring the bell so that the bus could move off while it was tantalisingly just out of reach? This trolleybus was one of the first to run in Huddersfield. The six wheeler AEC was the only such make in the initial batch, four of the others being

locally built by Karrier Motors. The first route to become operational was between Byram Street and Almondbury. Tram track renewal was expensive and the first nails in the tramway coffin were hammered in on 4 December 1933.

Top left: Slaithwaite is the inspirational setting for the fictional Skelthwaite, the base for ITV's schmaltzy drama series 'Where the heart is'. The 64 tram on the 4 route to the small town on Manchester Road was at the top of Chapel Hill. Behind it we can see the new extension to the Co-op building on the corner of Buxton Road and East Parade. The Slaithwaite tram had an unusual 'turret ' design and you can be forgiven for imagining a machine gunner being sited there to deal with the unruly elements in Milnsbridge as the car passed through! The world loved its trams and there is more nostalgia about this form of road transport than any other. They even inspired Judy Garland to sing the Oscar nominated 'Trolley song' in her 1944 movie, 'Meet me in St Louis'. It was 1 May 1937 when this pair of vehicles was pictured and the start of a week in which several memorable events took place elsewhere in the world. Margaret Mitchell, a complete unknown, won a Pulitzer Prize for the only book that she ever wrote. Since it was called 'Gone with

the wind' she probably had no need of a further source of income once the film rights were agreed. On 6 May, the giant airship Hindenburg exploded in a ball of fire as it attempted to land in New Jersey, thus realistically bringing to an end the role of airships in the field of public transport.

Above: Huddersfield used six wheeler trolleybuses on its routes and they were very popular with the general public, as instanced by the crowded double decks on the 531 running on the 73 route from Waterloo to Outlane. Seen here making the turn into Kirkgate from Castlegate, this form of transport was nicknamed by some as 'the whispering death'. Pedestrians had become used to hearing the clanking of approaching trams as they strolled across the road, giving them an audible warning of danger on the move. When trolleybuses came along there was just a gentle swish to be heard and many an unwary soul suddenly found many tons of metal heading his way. In the 1930s, Britain had one of the worst road safety records in Europe. Casualties were at an unacceptable level, leading to the introduction of a variety of legislative and informative measures to be introduced. The Highway Code was published, street lighting improved, electrified traffic lights erected, cats' eyes inserted into carriageways and children given advice in the schoolroom on how to cross the road and cycle with care. Belisha crossings appeared in town centres and the driving test made compulsory in 1935 for drivers who had not held a licence before 1 April 1934. Trolleybuses dominated public transport in and around town either side of the war, but the increased costs of electricity and equipment saw them phased out during the 1960s. The last vehicle ran on this very route on 13 July 1968.

Huddersfield started to run its own public transport service on 11 January 1883. It was the first example in Britain of a municipally operated tramway system. In other towns and cities Corporation-owned tracks were all leased to private enterprise. These early trams ran on steam, augmented for a few brief years by horse-drawn cars. Electrification took place in 1901 with the first services scheduled for conversion being Crosland Moor, Slaithwaite, Longwood, Outlane and the Lindley Circular route. This view of Westgate, across the Railway Street and Market Street junction, down to the distinctive Burton's building where John William Street meets Market Place, was taken in June 1950. The sky above the Plough Hotel and Whiteley's Café was criss-crossed with cabling used by trolleybuses. In the 1930s, as tram track renewal became increasingly expensive and when the track on the Almondbury route became due for replacement, the Tramways Committee decided to replace the trams with trolleybuses. The first trolleybus service in Huddersfield ran from Byram Street to Almondbury on 4 December 1933 using a fleet of six vehicles. The last tramcar ran to Brighouse on Saturday, 29 June 1940. The Huddersfield trolleybus system closed on 13th July 1968. All street trolleybus operation ceased in Britain when Bradford closed its service on the 26th March 1972. Since then, the only trolleybus operation in the UK has been in museums, such as the one at Sandtoft, halfway between Doncaster and Scunthorpe.

Below: How peaceful High Street looked in 1951. There was little traffic on the streets and the pace of life looks so much slower than the hurly burly rush we experience today. The middle of the last century was a tough time for everyone. The war years were only just behind us and the nation struggled to get back on its feet as the staggering cost of the battle against fascism was still crippling our economy. Towns and cities blasted apart in bombing raids had to be rebuilt. Investment in the nation's infrastructure had been put on hold as everything was geared up for the war effort and so private business and public sector development had been set back by years. It would take over a decade after hostilities ended before we could feel that we had turned the corner. Expectation was high in the immediate euphoria of the summer of 1945. A new government, under the leadership of Clement Attlee, swept to power, full of promises about doing away with the old order. The National Health Service was an immediate success, but the gathering of large industries and services into public control under a variety of nationalising moves was too much, too soon. Goods were still rationed in the shops and wages were not high enough to provide workers with more than the basics. When the pound was devalued by a stunning 30 per cent in 1949, the writing was on the wall for the government. At the general election in 1951, voters turned to Churchill once more.

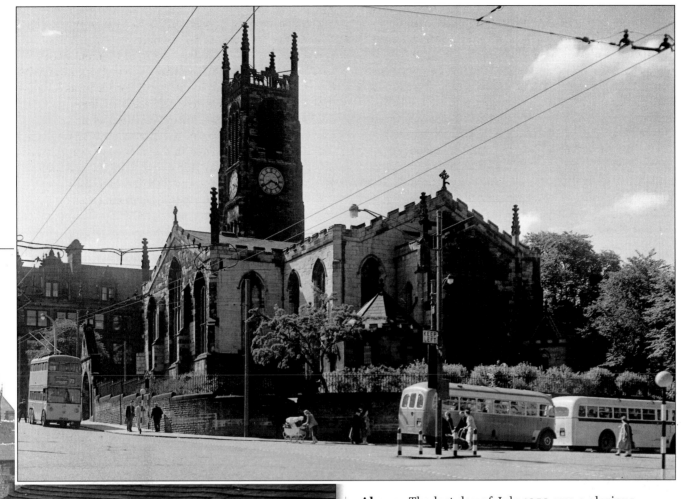

Above: The last day of July 1950 was a glorious, sunny occasion to take the baby out for a stroll in a Silver Cross pram with a little canopy to protect the youngster from the rays of summer that shone from an almost cloudless sky. The period is clearly defined by the trolley bus and, especially, the Belisha crossing on Lord Street. Studs accompanied the winking beacon, named for the transport minister of the mid 1930s, on the roadway to mark out the path pedestrians had to take across the road. It was a couple of years later that the zebra markings were introduced to help motorists spot the crossings more easily. We were at the midpoint of the century and everyone hoped that the second half would bring the peace and prosperity for which we had endured two world wars and a decade's worth of economic depression. Today was the one that saw Sainsbury's open its first self service store in Croydon. Surely, that little landmark marked the start of something new? Oh how naive we were. That very week, British troops were sent to Korea under the orders of the United Nations and, yet again, our brave lads were asked to give their lives on a foreign field for a cause that seemed, to the man in the street, of little concern to us at home. Prayers were offered in Kirkgate's St Peter's Parish Church, yet again.

Above: After the amalgamation in 1926 created ICI, its constituent companies produced chemicals, dyes, explosives, fertilisers, fibres, nonferrous metals and paints. The group went on to produce a wider range of chemicals, paints, pharmaceuticals, synthetic fibres (especially polyesters and nylon) and plastics. Outside the Leeds Road plant on 21 July 1955, workers were generally quite pleased with their lot. The country was coming out of the postwar doldrums and the economic situation was looking up. Pay packets were fatter than before and could stretch to buying such luxury items as a television, vacuum cleaner, fridge or washing machine. Not all at once of course, though buying things 'on tick' helped spread the load. Notice how the workforce was beginning to change its transport habits. Most still caught the bus home after work, or cycled back, but some had enough to spend on a motorbike or even a car. Pedestrians crossing the road used to shout, 'Who do you think you are, Geoff Duke/Reg Harris?' at motorbikers or cyclists who were threatening to run them down. Soon, the name changed to 'Stirling Moss' as more widespread ownership meant that the motorcar was not the preserve of the middle classes any more. In 1993, ICI split off its drug, pesticide and specialty chemical concerns into a new corporation named Zeneca Group plc. The parent company continued to produce industrial chemicals, paints and explosives.

Holmfirth is a delightful little town to the south of Huddersfield, providing a gateway over Woodhead into the Peak District. It has 20th century links with humour of both the saucy and whimsical genres. It was here, in 1903, that the Bamforth family begin producing postcards that were later to include the seaside varieties that depicted large busted ladies and blushing, hen pecked men underneath a risqué caption. Television audiences discovered Holmfirth via the long-running 'Last of the Summer Wine' and the town became a popular visiting place for coachloads of day trippers keen to see the café where Foggy and his pals put the world to rights or the hidden corner where Howard and Marina had

their trysts. Perhaps this photograph from early June 1953 shows Norah Batty in earnest conversation with Compo, though the young lady's stockings have yet to take on a wrinkled appearance. This view of Victoria Street, the road that takes visitors from the main Huddersfield Road and into the town square, was gaily decorated ready for the celebrations that were held to mark the coronation of Queen Elizabeth II. Gay bunting and Union Flags were everywhere as the nation rejoiced, seeing her time on the throne as being that of a new Elizabethan Age that would obliterate the austerity of the postwar era.

Above: It was a dank and dark October afternoon in 1956 as we look into Buxton Road from the crossroads, with High Street to the right and Ramsden Street to the left. The pair of flagpoles on the building on Ramsden Street belong to the Town Hall. It dates from 1881 and a civic service was held at St Peter's Parish Church on 18 October 1981 to mark its centenary. The Duke of Wellington's Regiment marched through the town and an organ recital was held, with an enactment of the original opening ceremony being carried out. All of the area leading away in front of us is now known as New Street and is part of the pedestrianised shopping area that has been with us for over 30 years. No cars, such as the baby Austin coming towards the camera, and the Morris Minor parked at the kerbside, have dared to drive along here since Harold Wilson had a second taste of life at 10 Downing Street. In the distance, the clock tower on the Co-op building can be seen at the junction with Chapel Hill. Although this time of the year was not anyone's favourite cup of tea, soccer fans noted some interesting developments at the Leeds Road ground that autumn. In November, a new manager was appointed. Not many had heard of Bill Shankly, but after four years of

management with Huddersfield Town he moved to Liverpool where he became a legendary figure. In December 1956, Shankly called up a 16 year old youngster from the reserves to make his debut in professional football on Christmas Eve at Notts County's Meadow Lane. The scrawny, squint eyed kid from Aberdeen went by the name of Denis Law, or 'The King' if you are a Manchester United fan.

Below left: Huddersfield's reputation and prosperity were built upon its successful textile industry. The boom in the town's economy helped provide the finance for some of the finest Victorian architecture seen anywhere in the country. The Prince of Wales, a controversial commentator on building design, was moved to comment, following a visit to Huddersfield, that the town centre and its approach road from Edgerton contained some of the most stunning architecture he had ever seen. The façade of the railway station is so attractive that it has led to the building being described as a 'stately home with trains in it'. Pictured opposite to it, across St George's Square, on 16 August 1956 are the magnificent premises of the Huddersfield Building Society. The society was formed following a series of meetings in the 1860s at Elm Crest, now a Grade II listed guest house just off the main Huddersfield to Halifax road. Building societies were formed for the mutual benefit of members wishing to invest and secure loans against the purchase of property. In more recent times, many of these have abandoned their mutual status and become fully fledged banks, much to the dismay of many of their members. The Huddersfield Building Society merged with the Bradford Permanent Building Society in 1975, becoming the Huddersfield and Bradford. A further merger took place with the West Yorkshire in 1982 creating the new Yorkshire Building Society, the third largest in the country.

Above: Napoleon once described England, in what he thought were derogatory terms, as a nation of shopkeepers. So what if we were? Long after Old Boney had been laid to rest, our little shops continued to trade quite happily. Even in the 21st century, there are still some examples left of corner shops plying their trade and serving the local community. Times and fashions may have changed, but some soldier on. Television's 'Coronation Street' mirrors some of those developments. Where once Florrie Lindley ran a small business, now it is Devindra and Sunita Alahan who hold the reins. This reflects true life where a large number of Asian families have taken over the role of the local shopkeeper. However, back in 1958, when we looked at the junction of Northgate and Northumberland Street, we can tell that we are truly in the time of Arkwright's 'Open All Hours' style of retail outlets. Older readers might recall some of the businesses here that included Ireland's, Cockcroft's chemist's, Eastman's butcher's, Swallow's newsagency, Hay's shoes, Ramsdale's greengrocer's and Kahn's rainwear. A real variety of shops was packed close together and was typical of the way our streets looked in the middle of the last century. All the property on Northgate was demolished to make way for the inner ring road. A piece of history and an example of our parents' lifestyle were swept away as well.

Above: The float was provided by Garrard's, the timber merchants from Great Northern Street, as part of the parade held in the 1950s to honour the sacrifices made by members of the armed forces during World War I. It was emblazoned with British Legion slogans, 'Service not self' and 'From Flanders fields we were born'. Old soldiers from the Great War, as it was originally known, must have wondered how it was that the world had ignored the lessons learned from their time in uniform. How else could great powers have allowed the same carnage to take place again just over 20 years after Armistice Day? Douglas Haig, the British Army's commander in chief, was heavily criticised for his policies that led to huge numbers of casualties. After the war, perhaps to make some amends, he helped organise the British Legion and travelled throughout the Empire, collecting money for needy ex servicemen. Garrard's set up its business during that war when Stanley Garrard and a colleague, a certain Mr Eastwood, went into partnership.

Below: Lorries and trailers were pressganged into service during the 1958 Honley Carnival. This Albion Clansman, seen at Moorbottom, was just one of many that were garlanded with flowers and bedecked with colourful streamers ready to take part in the parade. Local firms gave generously to the event, inspired by a mixture of philanthropy and advertising acumen. Tableaux depicting such diverse subjects as characters from children's literature, historical events or international culture often provided the theme for the carnival procession. They also included the 'must' for any show, that of the carnival queen accompanied by her attendants. Little lads, with well scrubbed faces and slickly Brilliantined hair, were kitted out in page boy suits. Their disgust and embarrassment was in direct proportion to the pride shown on their mothers' faces. Little girls, selected to be handmaidens, put on the prettiest of white dresses, but could only swallow their disappointment in playing second fiddle to the one chosen to be queen for a day. She was the centre of attention as the procession swept through the streets where crowds of local families watched this display of British traditional celebration. In most cases, the carnival was the equivalent of a pagan fertility festival, but that connection was somewhat tenuous by the middle of the 20th century. By then it had become just a fixture in the calendar when there was an opportunity to enjoy a special Saturday and round off the festivities with a show and a funfair.

Eastwood's association was short-lived and, eventually, the business passed into the hands of Stanley's son, Geoffrey, until he perished in a sailing accident on Lake Windermere. The managing director, Derek Stott, then bought out the business though he retained the Garrard name as it had gained a formidable reputation for reliability and quality.

Right: The A629 Edgerton Road and New North Road is the main link from Halifax into Huddersfield. The roadsign pointing right heads traffic from Blacker Road along Edgerton Grove Road towards the A640 that heads off over the border to Denshaw. This crossroads, photographed in 1956, is only a few hundred yards from the town, yet it still looks today much the same as it was 50 years ago. The shadows cast by the tall trees continue to dapple the roadway and the bushes look glorious in summertime when the flowers are in bloom. The property along this road is all well constructed. Large houses and long driveways are features here. The opulent grandeur of these homes illustrates that the wealthy lived here and, in many cases, still do. Although a number of these buildings have now been turned into offices or partitioned into flats, there continue to be many that still belong to families with a bob or two to their names. Perhaps the only real difference here relates to the traffic flow. Instead of the occasional van on the move, as depicted here, the road is now busy at most times of the day. Rush hour is a bumper to bumper affair as traffic moves, albeit slowly, to and from the M62 link at Ainley Top.

Bottom left: There is no longer a need for traffic lights at this New Street junction with High Street, to the right, and Ramsden Street, out of shot to the left. The area now forms part of the pedestrianised centre of Huddersfield retail life. Shoppers can happily walk in safety along what was Buxton Road until town planners decided to rename it. There must have been much scratching of heads and tremendous effort by various think tanks before the marvellously imaginative name of 'New Street' was determined. No doubt the sons and daughters of such intellectuals will rename New Street as 'Even Newer Street' in the next phase of remodelling. These High Street buildings, dating from 1935, that dominate the street corner are still with us. In 1959, the tobacconist advertised Capstan cigarettes for sale. This was a powerful brand, not for the fainthearted. Only a seasoned smoker could manage to remain standing after a Capstan full strength before breakfast. Lesser mortals turned pale at the gills. Klick, a photo developing service, has its premises here today. To the left, an art supplies shop has replaced the Red Circle Library and Gregg's bakery is now to the right. Just to the left of this photograph there is now an alley leading into Albion Street named Buxton Way, one small attempt to retain a link with the road's former name.

Below: We have long been known as a nation of animal lovers and there is hardly a home in the land that has not had some form of pet living there at some time. Mallinson's on King Street was happy to supply all the creature comforts Fido or Tiddles could want for a cold nose and glossy coat in the late 1950s. Of course, it was not just dogs and cats that were brought into our houses. Whistling budgerigars became very popular, especially with the elderly who had not got the time or mobility to walk the dog. Caged creatures even managed, later on, to inspire Rotherham's Duggie Brown to come up with a joke about an old lady, a parrot and a plumber. This long-winded tale helped keep his career on track for another 35 years! Other pet lovers who also wanted something that did not require exercising went in for tropical fish. Some spent a fortune on heated tanks, special plants and Siamese fighting fish, only to find them floating on top of the water within the week. Children always pestered for a rabbit or hamster and, of course, the parents gave in under the interminable pressure, even if they knew that it would be they who soon would have to do the mucking out. Notice the flat dweller above the Famous Army Stores. One of those new fangled television sets was obviously a proud possession as an aerial poked its lonely bars skywards.

Above: By the 1960s and 1970s nearly all the towns in Britain were bedevilled with the problem of dealing with the huge rise in car ownership. What had once been limited to the middle classes was now a commonplace possession. Our roads and town centres could not cope. Congested streets and snarled up shopping areas became commonplace. All manner of measures were introduced, including one way systems, multi storey car parks, pedestrianisation and parking meters, but still the problem escalated. It was not helped by through traffic negotiating town centres as it attempted to move to more distant destinations. Consequently, ring roads and by-passes proliferated.

Queensgate, seen here in 1971, is part of the ring road that was officially opened by Alderman Whittaker on 2 November 1973. A close look at the individuals in this photograph reveals that the young man with the briefcase and the pair of teenage boys are of Asian appearance. The increasing numbers of immigrants from the Asian sub-continent over the last 40 years has led to a cultural mix in our town that is far different from that experienced by our parents or grandparents. The integration and acceptance of a changing society has not been easy for either the host or the newcomer though much has been done for which both can feel proud

Below: David Lockwood, hair stylist, operated a business behind the net curtains on the floor above Sharps on Market Street. He would have been busy crimping and setting as more mature ladies had their regular session under the dryer. Younger lasses wanted cuts with flicked up ends like Sandie Shaw or piled up tresses a la Dusty Springfield. Girls were very keen to follow their own fashion trends and were not interested in just being newer versions of their mothers. The mini skirt was all the rage and hemlines became more like pelmets. Dry cleaners started to charge twopence an inch for their services and dad's blood pressure rose in direct proportion to the height above the knee to which his daughter's mini climbed. This photograph was taken on 8 June 1968 when Gary Puckett and the Union Gap were warbling 'Young Girl' at the top of the charts. This song, about a man's attraction for a Lolita-style of temptress, somehow escaped a ban by the BBC. Usually, 'Auntie' saw itself as a keeper of public morals and went to town on anything with a suggestive or overtly sexual lyric. The following year it banned 'Je t'aime' by Serge Gainsbourg and Jane Birkin and even as late as 1983 was pulling the plug on such as Frankie Goes to Hollywood's 'Relax'.

At leisure

And the brass band played, tiddly om, pom-pom. In June 1956 the procession wound its way through Rawthorpe as part of the annual Children's Treat. Pretty girls clutched nosegays and bouquets as they sat in the decorated floats, while their proud mums smiled with the self satisfaction that each one had the most beautiful and best turned out daughter in all of Huddersfield. Each of them, in her own eyes, was quite correct. Elsewhere, youngsters tucked into proper ice cream cornets and wafers. They were the real stuff, not the whippy, machine fed apology for an ice cream that we now suffer. This was the real stuff, carefully prepared in a dairy and sent out in large refrigerated tubs to be scooped from the vat in a van into a cone and topped with tasty raspberry. Wafers were dispensed via a special rectangular tool and lolly lovers could drool over an Orange Maid, that 'drink on a stick'. Other favourites included the Pemberton's Twicer. 'What could be nicer than a Pemberton's Twicer - ice cream with a lolly each end?' Simple tastes, but exotic pleasures were garnered from such straightforward treats. As children we ran after the van, with its tannoy tinkling out a tune, to ask the driver if he had any broken wafers he could let us have for free. Happy days.

Left: ICI is a major British corporation that was founded in 1926 as Imperial Chemicals Industries when four major British chemical companie - Brunner, Mond and Company, Nobel Industries, United Alkali and the British Dyestuffs Corporation - all amalgamated under one banner. The company acknowledged the need for a happy workforce and soon instituted a series of family treats, that including special children's events. This one took place at the Palace Theatre in 1953. Actors and entertainers came into the auditorium to meet the children and thrill them by letting them see their costumes and make-up at close quarters. Over half a century on, those happy, smiling faces that we can see here will, in many cases, be grannies and grandpas by now. They fondly recall the days when they sat in these rows at the Palace and shouted their heads off at the antics on stage and cheered their approval of the 'turns' who came to entertain them. How those of us who were there in those days love to relive those memories through the eyes and ears of our own grandchildren, as we separate them from their abysmal Game Boys and Play Stations and take them to the pantomime at Christmas. It is a sheer delight to boo the villain and cheer the heroine, as well as chuckle at jokes that have whiskers on them.

Below: Southern softies, such as Michael Winner, think that it is 'grim up north'. It is all flat hats, ferrets and black peas. The only culture to be found is that grown on the mould found on the walls of damp, grimy back-to-back terraces. Of course, the only music is that played on a pair of spoons. Those blinkered souls south of Watford Gap have never attempted to take in the mellifluous music of a north country brass band. The pursed lips and dextrous fingers of cornet, trumpet and euphonium players can help emit the most delightful renditions of military marches, light classics and songs from the shows. The art of bandsmen, old and young, is something nurtured in every town and village across Yorkshire and, dare we say it, Lancashire. Many brass bands, such as the internationally renowned Black Dyke Mills Band, were initially associated with businesses. Others grew from a common community interest. We have even had success in the pop music charts, as when the Brighouse and Rastrick band got to No 2 in 1977. But for Paul McCartney's 'Mull of Kintyre' selling 2 million copies, 'The Floral Dance' would have topped the pops that Christmas. In 1952, Guiseley Silver Band waited its turn to play in a competition held at Huddersfield Town Hall. Some of the younger lads in the photograph may have only just hung up their instruments because of advancing years. That would be the only reason, as they never became 'brassed off' with the music.

Below: Up, up and away, but not in a beautiful balloon. The view was gained from a cage on the end of a lorry's hydraulic arm. The health and safety snoopers of today would be apoplectic at such a sight and only too happy to reach for their clipboards to write out a 'Stop' notice or have the perpetrators clapped in irons. In the 21st century the only risk that can be taken in our lives is in the form of a board game. Fortunately, back in June 1960, the nanny state had not been born and we were allowed to have some fun and be permitted a degree of exhilaration. This little family group, high above the crowds, was housed on the Simon Platform owned by ICI. This company was, at the time, Huddersfield's biggest single employer, with over 5,000 employees owing their livelihood to the firm. The management took its position as a caring employer very seriously and looked after its staff and families. The annual children's gala was always a treat

to be eagerly anticipated. It looks from this evidence that flaming June had lived up to its reputation, if the number of summery frocks is any guide. Floral prints and swirling, just below the knee hemlines were the order of the day. There were sideshows, races and lots of ice cream to be enjoyed and, boy, didn't we just?

Above: The Americans can have their Independence Day but no thoughts about our cousins in that former colony of ours entered the minds of those enjoying themselves at the Hopkins Lane gala day on 4 July 1959. We were lucky with the weather, as the sun beat down all day. Little girls in summer frocks and little dresses, with ankle length white socks sticking through peek-a-boo sandals, sat with their mums or on dad's knee engrossed in what was happening in front of them. Boys, too, hair close cropped and with knees that you could actually see beneath their short trousers, looked equally as transfixed with the entertainment unfolding in front of their eyes. We can only guess as to what it was that captured their attention. Perhaps there was a dancing display or a brass band playing. Best of all would have been a Punch and Judy show, full of sausages and mayhem that delighted audiences for donkey's years before the politically correct loonies decided that such fun bred a hooligan culture in our offspring and sowed the seeds for wife beaters of the future. It has yet to be proved that any violent criminal shouted 'That's the way to do it' as he mugged some poor soul in the middle of Ramsden Street. Those enjoying their time at the gala were more interested in having a laugh than in some deeply psychological, social research.

Events & occasions

Below: This incongruous group was seen outside Moxon Mills on a summer's day in 1950. The ladies seemed rather bored with proceedings and only the bright sunshine is giving them any sort of pleasure. However, history does not relate what it was that caused them to wish that they were a million miles away. The members of the armed forces look similarly puzzled as they probably had better things to do, as well. When the textile bubble burst, many of these old mills fell derelict. Fortunately, others were rescued and continue to serve a useful purpose today. A large number became warehouses or were turned into homes for businesses selling a variety of retail goods. Elsewhere, property developers recognised a gap in the housing market and, inspired by the reclamation of buildings in the London and Manchester docklands, began refurbishing the old mills. They were completely remodelled into luxury apartments, attracting many young couples and upwardly mobile singles anxious to get a foot on the property ladder. These people have little interest in gardening and other traditional accompaniments to house dwelling and are more than happy to exchange these for a guaranteed parking place and a modest service charge. The old mills, many of which were once sweat shops where people hated working, became homes that others love.

Right: As well as the usual streamers on sticks and union flags, one woman proudly held a large version of the Red Ensign, the Merchant Navy's 'red duster'. Perhaps her hubby had served nobly in the convoys during the war and she had this emblem as a proud reminder of his days of duty on perilous seas. There is a delightful mixture of footwear to be seen on display by this

group. There seems to be almost every type imaginable, including open toed sandals, court shoes, pumps and patent leather high heels. However, pride of place must go to the lady on the right with the clogs. She made sure that her fashion ensemble was complete by firmly clutching that most necessary of women's accessories, the handbag. This happy band of workers was standing outside ICI on Leeds Road. They had abandoned their duties as canteen staff to welcome Princess Elizabeth and Prince Philip on their official visit to the town in July 1949. The royal couple was on its way to the town's football stadium where 8,000 children waited to greet them. This was part of a three day visit to the West Riding that also took in a stop off at Trafalgar Mills on Leeds Road where fine worsted fabrics were manufactured.

Above: We must have run out of flags in April 1953, or perhaps we were saving them for the coronation in June. It was most unusual for a royal visit not to be marked by little flags on sticks being waved furiously by children as if their very lives depended upon it. Princess Margaret was no ordinary Windsor, either. Her sister had become our monarch the previous February when their father, George VI, passed away, so this was a woman of substance. Families waited patiently and police officers passed the time of day with each other as they waited for the princess to emerge from her limousine. When she at last appeared there was a huge cheer that could be heard all the way across town. Margaret was a lively soul and one whose activities had started to interest the popular newspapers. She was something of a rebellious and forthright person, as second children often are, and soon made her way into the gossip columns with her comments

and social whirl. She had curtailed some of her activities of late out of respect for her grandmother, Queen Mary. This grand old lady, the widow of George V, died some three weeks before this visit and Margaret was still observing a period of mourning whilst continuing to carry out her official duties.

Below left: Lots and lots of happy smiling faces squashed together outside the walls surrounding the parish church. People were used to crowding near here as, for many years, the area in front of the church was used as a bus terminus. The churchyard that became St Peter's Gardens was once full to almost literally bursting. By 1850 some 38,000 bodies were at rest there, meaning that new graves were often dug at the same time as exposing old ones. Not a pretty sight! It came as no surprise when a new cemetery at Edgerton was commissioned. The church itself was built in 1836 on the site of one that dated back to the early years of the 16th century. Pritchett, the architect, went on to design the railway station, one of Huddersfield's most magnificent structures. Those in the crowd were not too interested in religious or architectural history, though they did possess a sense of tradition. A visit from Princess Margaret, just six weeks before her sister's coronation, was an important occasion worthy of note. Mums, in partic-

ular, turned out in droves to catch a glimpse of what the modern, privileged miss was wearing. The few men who turned up were not to be disappointed, either. They may not have bothered about hemlines or tucks and pleats, and the only darts that interested them were thrown at the pub, but they knew a pretty girl when they saw one.

Above: There are some bored faces on view, especially paraded by the boys, as the lone bobby on hand controlled this segment of the crowd when Princess Margaret arrived on 18 April 1953. How different it would be today. We would have huge barriers to keep us back, rows of uniforms standing in front of us, goodness knows what sort of metal detectors and security screens, closed circuit cameras watching our every move and no chance of getting close to the honoured guest. She came to attend a special service at St Peter's conducted by the curate, Reverend David Shepherd. He was a sportsman of note and even went to the top of the cricketing tree as a Test match batsman of some style. Later, he was to become the Anglican Bishop of Liverpool. Princess Margaret was destined to live in the shadow of her sister, but still had to conform to the strict mores laid down by royal advisers. It was her affair with Group Captain Peter Townsend that was to move her onto the front pages in 1955 when it seemed certain that she was going to announce marriage to her father's former equerry. He was a divorced man and the establishment feared ructions that might rival the 1936 abdication crisis. She eventually gave in to the pressure and severed connections with Townsend, but was never to find lasting happiness.

St Joseph's Church May Day procession took place in Raglan Road on 4 May 1958. The road was so named for Baron Raglan (1788-1855), the British forces' commander in chief during the Crimean War who died at Sebastopol. It was his ambiguous order that led to the heroic, but disastrous, Charge of the Light Brigade. The Victorians named many of their streets after wartime heroes, hence the large proliferation of Nelsons and Gordons in Britain's A to Z books. A surprise guest to the procession turned up, much to the delight of the crowd and consternation of the police and St John Ambulance workers concerned about the crush caused by fans and wellwishers. The glamorous blonde, fur stole and peroxide hair to the fore, is instantly recognisable as the unfortunately named Diana Mary Fluck (1931-84). Though stereotyped as a postwar good time girl, she was more, bringing talent and sensuality to the British cinema, as well as driving men wild with her mink bikini. The railway town of Swindon was an unprepossessing start for a starlet, but Diana loved film from the age of three. Her mother lavished her with gifts and her father begrudgingly sent her to the best private schools. Physically and socially mature for her age, Diana became a pinup girl at 13. She lied to the photographers and later directors, claiming she was 17. By the time she started out in the acting world, she had become Diana Dors, Britain's answer to Marilyn Monroe.

Above: This was not quite 'Proms in the Park', but the interest generated was just as keen as any highbrow entertainment London might put on. The grounds around the open air theatre at Greenhead Park were packed on 11 July 1953 as spectators enjoyed a talent show, hoping to spot some future star in the making. Perhaps Roy Castle, the all round entertainer from Scholes, might have tried his luck here. The entertainment in the park was a throwback to the war years when people were encouraged to join in the 'Holidays at Home' scheme. The government, conscious of keeping public morale high during those difficult times, knew that traditional holidays at the seaside were impossible for most of us. Rationing and the requisitioning of transport for use by the armed forces meant that we were forced to stay put. To soften the blow, local councils were encouraged to organise activities in local parks and stadiums so that the general public could enjoy some fun without going out of town. These events were so popular that they were continued into peacetime. This talent show had obviously captured the imagination of Huddersfield folk as the audience looked on with rapt attention. There were children tap dancing, singers belting out 'How much is that doggie in the window', comedians with the corniest of jokes, ventriloquists whose lips moved and banjo players plucking minstrel tunes in a true variety show.

KD Decoratives - Christmas every day

Christmas is a magical time. But to make magic work, you need, a magician. Since the 1970s Richard and Gloria Kitchen-Dunn have been making magic with their Christmas decorations. While most of us have a box of Christmas decorations tucked away for Yuletide they have hundreds of fantastical Christmas figures, thousands of feet of tinsel and millions of baubles.

When Richard was eight, the family was living in Chelsea at the height of the London blitz. A whistling-bomb fell in the street in front of their home while they shivered in an Anderson shelter in the back garden.

Though the bomb did not explode, it caused extensive damage, and for the next few weeks the family slept on mattresses in churches and underground stations.

Along with their three sons Jamie, David and Matthew and their families, the couple spend the whole year designing, making and preparing everything for one of the largest festive decorating jobs in the world - lavishly bedecking dozens of shopping centres with Christmas displays.

Today the Huddersfield firm of KD Decoratives Ltd. is one of Europe's leading suppliers of seasonal displays. Everything is assembled under one roof: scenery, giant animated figures, props, lighting, special effects, computerised shows and costumes.

Visiting the premises of KD Decoratives is a treat in itself. A Toyland train takes clients on a ride through a Christmas wonderland complete with Santa Claus, reindeer, snowmen, elves, goblins and a complete cast of fairytale characters.

Many of the displays feature animatronics, allowing the festive characters to move, talk and sing. The displays have been provided to customers as diverse as Disneyland Paris, Alton Towers and London's Natural History Museum. In the 21st century the company has been doing more business overseas, with a band of animatronic giant teddy bears sent to enchant visitors in a theme park in Hong Kong.

If it all sounds like a theatre show, it's no wonder. It's in the KD blood.

Richard Kitchen-Dunn was born in Cleethorpes in 1934. His mother and father were on the stage, and the family would spend three or four months in different towns, his parents entertaining in clubs and small theatres before moving on.

The bombing prompted a move to the house of Richard's grandmother in Bradford, before moving on to Sheffield two years later.

School in Sheffield was the first time that Richard and his brother had any continuity of education. At school Richard discovered a love of football and boxing, the latter very quickly stopped the bullying that he received for not having a proper Yorkshire accent.

Richard had three part-time jobs after school: delivering groceries each day, as well as daily morning and Sunday paper rounds.

By the age of 14 he had saved up enough money to buy his first bicycle, made to his personal specifications. It cost what was then the extraordinary sum of one hundred pounds. He would set off on his own and think nothing of doing 150 miles in a day.

At 16 Richard signed for Leeds United Juniors football team, training twice a week at Elland Road. Although he didn't get many games, (there were too many other youngsters) he did, however, get to play with the great John Charles.

Leaving school at 15, Richard's first job was working for the Sporting Pink in Leeds as a copy boy. His father, however, thought he should have an apprenticeship, so

Top: Founders Richard and Gloria Kitchen-Dunn.
Right: A Bendix Window display designed by Richard Kitchen-Dunn - winner of the Bendix 1967 World Window Display competition (32 countries entered).

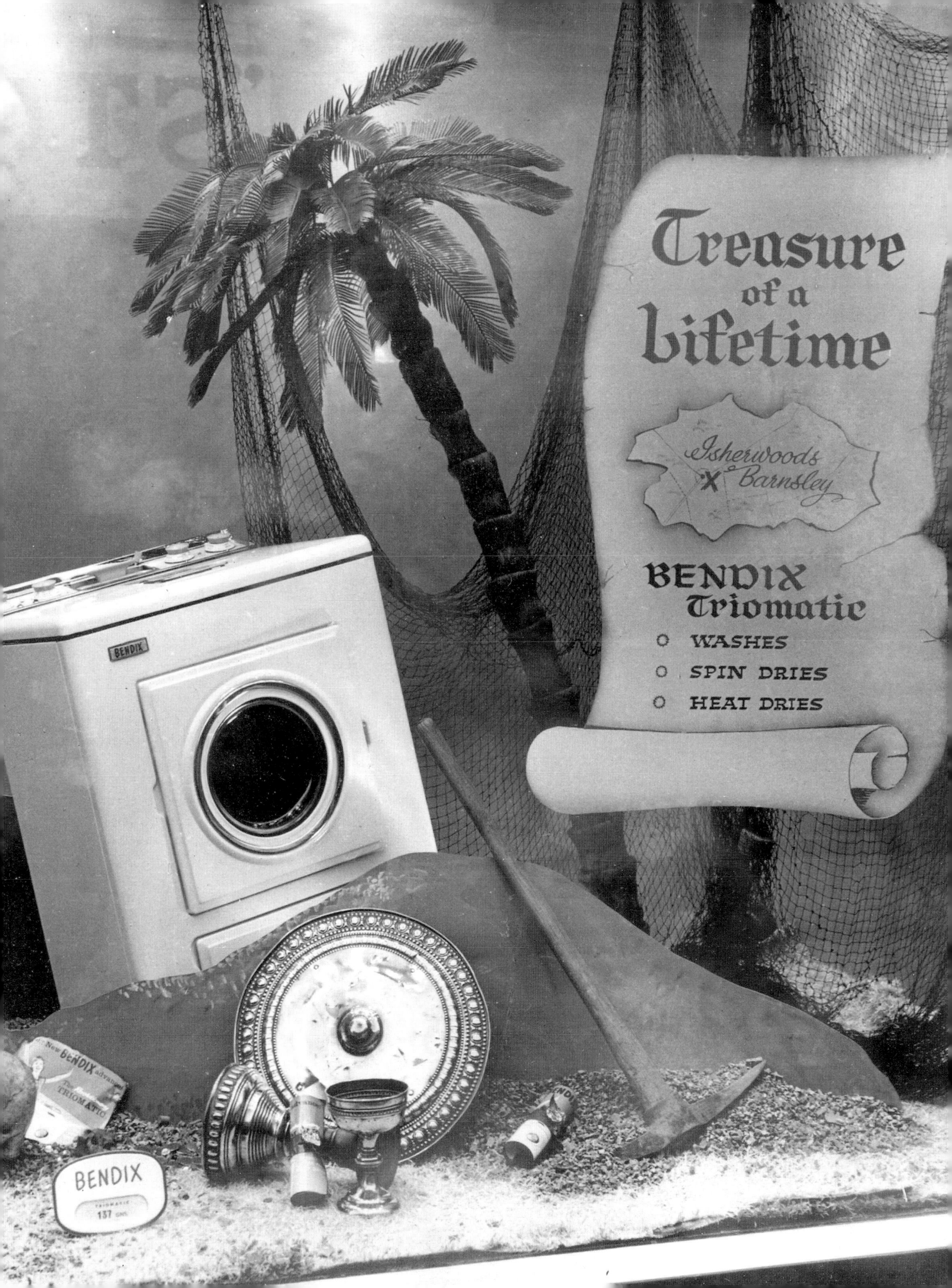

Treasure
of a
lifetime

Isherwoods X Barnsley

BENDIX Triomatic
○ WASHES
○ SPIN DRIES
○ HEAT DRIES

BENDIX
137 cm.

Richard went to work at Leeds General Infirmary in the electrical department. The position didn't last long: the course involved studying maths - not Richard's strong point.

National Service came next. Those who joined for three years rather than the usual two could choose their trade. Richard joined the RAF for three years as a Physical Training Instructor. It took him 14 months to get his tapes as a corporal before being posted to Flying Training Command to keep officers fit.

When Richard came out of the forces he was 21. He found a job as a printer's labourer at John Waddington's, feeding the presses with card and paper. At this time Richard was living in Stourton on the outskirts of Leeds. He enjoyed singing in close harmony, a talent inherited from his parents, aunts, uncles and grandparents (all of whom had been music hall performers). Together with a friend, Richard entered a talent competition at the Empire Theatre in Leeds, organised by Canadian impresario Carol Levis. The pair won the competition and went on to become semi-professionals. They worked for Carol Levis doing weekly and summer seasons at Blackpool and Morecambe, as well as getting work on BBC Television and radio.

To his father's disappointment however, Richard quit show-business. Looking for a better job, he dressed up and went to see the manager of Vallance's store in Leeds and asked him for a job as a salesman. Martin Vallance, the managing director, was impressed and offered him a three-month trial.

Art had been Richard's best subject at school, but he had never realised that this would come in useful for window dressing. After a few months Richard was helping the firm's window dresser and cheerfully offering him advice. He had found his niche in life.

Martin Vallance, and his father, the company Chairman, were so impressed that they offered Richard the job of Display Manager, travelling around the country, dressing all the firm's shop windows - doubling his wage to £1,200 a year, plus a company car. To earn over a thousand pounds a year in 1961 was something, especially in window dressing.

Richard went on to win many awards before being headhunted by Alwyn Isherwoods where he was impressed by the window display put on by a young lady named Gloria in the record department. Richard asked the company if she could work with him. Two years later they were married.

Then followed a brief period of being a self-employed window dresser, followed by five years employed with another display company: the last two years being spent as a director of the firm. However, Richard still hankered to work for himself.

Though KD Decoratives Ltd. started out in a very small way in 1977, it is certainly big business now. One of the largest tasks came in 2002, the year the company celebrated its 25th anniversary. The order was part of a £10 million children's ride being created at Manchester's

Top: A window display designed for Lewis's, Leeds.

Trafford Centre. *'Dreamieland'* featured animated robotic figures of 'Dreamie' and 'Dream Guzzlers' - the goodies and baddies.

Families on the ride would sit in one of ten fibreglass cars created by KD Decoratives and pass through nine zones on a five minute trip, during which time they would be invited to try and zap the Guzzlers with computerised guns.

KD Decoratives was asked to design and manufacture some 140 moving figures. The job would be the largest and most complex ever undertaken by the family run firm. Parts made in Huddersfield were taken to Manchester on a fleet of 20 lorries.

A total of 180 blocks of polystyrene, each measuring 8ft by 4ft by 2 ft were used for sculpting the features and characters. The production phase took six months, followed by three months of installation. 25 full-time sculptors, artists and engineers worked on the job, plus a team of five computer experts who wrote the software to animate the characters.

Anyone visiting the company's showrooms will feel like they have just stepped into Neverland, returning to a child's world of fantasy. Banjo-playing bears, singing oak trees, dancing teddies, cola drinking polar bears and talking reindeer are just some of the characters used in Christmas displays all over the country.

Since it began in the 1970s Christmas has started in October each year for the Kitchen-Dunn family.

When KD Decoratives began, one of the main raw materials was tinsel imported from the Far East. It was not very sophisticated, nor really made for the display market, being more intended for domestic use. Richard and Gloria had to re-design most of the items and get the manufacturers to build larger units.

Left: *The company's first grotto in the Manchester Arndale.* **Below:** *The first KD Decoratives showroom.*

Their son Matthew had the idea of creating animated characters. He was always interested in computers and animation and felt the family firm could use his talents.

Matthew's interest in animatronics inspired him to invent the company's first intricate animation system in 1987 after he fell 30 feet while decorating a store, braking both his arms. The designs he made during his convalescence would ensure that reindeer could eventually gallop on the spot, that gnomes could hammer away at their lasts and that Santa could 'ho ho ho' in time to the ever present seasonal music.

The family started the new aspect of the business in the garage of their home, with another of the Kitchen-Dunn sons, David, who wrote and recorded the music to be used with the displays.

The first animated Christmas grotto appeared in 1987; based on the Wind in the Willows. Three years later, the family was counting Hamley's amongst its customers: the world's most famous toy shop in London's Regent Street. Now, by using near-silent running compressors and the latest pneumatic developments, the company has developed figures which display near human capabilities. KD Decoratives' own specially designed computer enables characters to be programmed and re-programmed for any event.

Since it was founded, KD Decoratives Ltd has emerged as leaders in the field. The firm had now moved into Huddersfield town centre in Estate Buildings with 1,000 square feet of space. Three years later the company moved again to Bath Mills in Albert Street, Lockwood. KD Decoratives is still based in the mill measuring 83,000 square feet, a building now owned by subsidiary company KD Properties Ltd; the firm also occupies

Above, both pictures: *A woodland and a circus display, just two examples of the magical scenes created by KD Decoratives.*

40,000 square feet in another building nearby. The showrooms occupy 12,000 square feet and feature an ever-changing display of animation and Christmas decorations: probably the largest of its kind in Europe.

Each stage of production from concept and design, through to the manufacture and dressing of the characters is carried out in Huddersfield. The displays are supplied to theme parks, television, film, theatre, exhibitions, shopping centres and department stores all over the world. Clients include Harrods, a shopping centre in Dubai and a theme park in Norway as well as museums and P&O cruise ships.

KD Decoratives are also proud to have designed and installed decorations for the Trafford Centre in Manchester over the last several years, including a stunning scheme featuring the famous 'Trafford Bears' animatronic characters.

Perhaps one of the most unusual sales has been that of supplying Christmas trees to the United Arab Emirates. That year, ex-pats and tourists visiting the WAFI shopping centre in Dubai could see an animated Santa Claus, complete with reindeer and polar bears: the whole scene topped off with two Christmas trees. The following year youngsters in Dubai found themselves learning the story of Cinderella thanks to KD Decoratives, while Sheffield's Meadowhall Shopping Centre was kitted out with giant pandas.

The company works right through the night from the beginning of October until November putting up the displays all over the UK and Ireland. Yet although Christmas may be their most important market, it is far from being the only aspect to the business. 'Fat Sam,' for example, was one of five animated characters created for a

display at an American-style diner in Edinburgh. The company used the latest animatronic techniques to create four full-size 1930s vintage gangsters and a New York policeman for the display. The £160,000 contract took KD Decoratives' staff two months to complete. Local folk may have wondered exactly who was responsible for producing Big G and Ma G the larger-than-life mascots of the Huddersfield Giants RLFC: wonder no more. KD Decoratives was made Kirklees Business of the Year in 2003. By then the company was also celebrating: they landed a Christmas contract with Westfield Shoppingtowns, the largest shopping centre company in the world, based in Australia and owners of malls in the USA, Australia, New Zealand and the United Kingdom.

The year 2003 would also see KD Decoratives staff travelling as far as Chile and the Caribbean to complete work on half a dozen P&O Christmas cruise liners. Amongst its recent projects KD Decoratives has supplied animated displays for a miniature bottle museum in Oslo and has also secured a three-year contract to provide Christmas displays at Manchester Airport.

From just two workers at its inception, today the company employs up to 90 staff. Richard Kitchen-Dunn is Chairman and Sales Director, Gloria is Company Secretary and Chief Designer, Jamie takes care of sales and design, David: sales, music and showroom design, Matthew: sales and animation while daughter-in-law Claire designs Christmas decorations.

'Small enough to care, big enough to cope' according to Richard Kitchen-Dunn. To which might be added '...and Huddersfield's very own magicians'.

Top left: The 'Fat Sam' character, one of five animated characters created for display at an American-style diner in Edinburgh. Below: From left to right: Jamie, Matthew and David Kitchen-Dunn.

Bird's eye view

Flying high above the town centre on 6 June 1960, some 16 years after the Normandy landings on D-Day, the photographer aimed his camera lens rather than a bomb sight on the town below. The aircraft was almost directly above where Huddersfield University now stands. Queen Street and Wakefield Road, the latter now part of the ring road as Southgate, lead north into town on the right of the photograph. The forked section, bottom left, shows Manchester Road meeting with Buxton Road before crossing town, via John William Street, to pass under the railway arches and off in the general direction of Fartown and Netheroyd Hill. Towards the top left of this town centre scene, we can pick out the attractive square that is St George's. Here we are proud to have one of the finest examples of Victorian railway station architecture ever to be created. Now a Grade I listed building, it dates from 1850. Architect JP Pritchett must have been proud of his work, but never could have imagined that his place in Huddersfield history would inspire a late 20th century poet laureate such as John Betjeman to wax lyrically on his design. He knew a thing or two about architectural beauty, writing once over, 'Come friendly bombs and rain on Slough'.

Smoke belching from cooling towers to the north and factory chimneys to the south show that Huddersfield was a town dependent upon its old industries even as late in the last century as 7 December 1960. The new ring road had still to be built, but by the end of the decade it would have made its mark on the scene below, though its full completion did not happen until 1973. Queen Street, entering bottom right and running up to King Street where it becomes Cross Church Street, was cut in two by the part of the new road that was to be designated as Queensgate. This happened alongside the site of St Paul's Church, seen here in the mid right of the photograph. Queensgate now runs off to the right from there to meet Wakefield Road by Kingsgate Shopping Centre, built to the right of this picture. The road junction at the lower left edge is where Queensgate now meets Manchester Road and Chapel Hill. Nearly half a century ago this was a major entry point into town for cross Pennine traffic. The traffic, heavy for 1960 as illustrated here, flowed in along the A62 and A616 into Buxton Road (New Street). The major part of this road that now lies within the boundary of the ring road was pedestrianised in the mid 70s.

This aerial shot was taken looking north across the town centre towards Fartown and Fixby as the railway line curves its way east in the general direction of Deighton and Colne Bridge. The junction at Chapel Hill that includes Manchester Road is in the left foreground, with Queen Street South over to the right. Just higher up from this latter junction, the old St Paul's Church can be seen on the bend on Queensgate. This site is now home to St Paul's Concert Hall. From here, Queen Street and Cross Church Street run up towards the parish church in the centre of the photograph. The magistrates' courts and police station stand out quite clearly as the lighter coloured buildings on the lower left. The roads leading out from the town, towards the top of the picture, are heading off towards Elland, Brighouse and Bradford. These days they would be aiming for intersections with the M62, but on 2 August 1968 the trans Pennine route was limited to the A62 and A640. On the day that the pilot flew over Huddersfield, Sirhan Sirhan was in court in Los Angeles, facing trial for the murder of Robert Kennedy, the favourite for the Democrat presidential nomination in the American elections that year. The 60s may have swung, but they were also violent times with assassinations and the Vietnam War forever on the front pages.

The tram coming down Buxton Road in the early 1930s was plying the route from Marsden to Bradley. Route 4 including cars that assisted the Post Office. Collaboration with the GPO began as far back as 20 March 1893 when some of the old steam trams were fitted with letter boxes on the front, just like the one carried by the 127 seen here. Huddersfield was one of the leading pioneers in this method of mail collection and delivery and one that it is remarkable to think did not have more universal appeal. During the 1920s our trams carried more post than all of those in the rest of the country put together. They even offered a Sunday collection, something that the Royal Mail vans have not been able to do for years. The tram postal service, which was of great benefit to the general public, continued right up to the outbreak of the second world war. The view along one of Huddersfield's busiest shopping areas shows that there were plenty of people out and about. However, not everyone we can see had money to burn. This was the era of the Depression when wages were low, jobs scarce and unemployment, at one stage, topped 3,000,000. Men became increasingly desperate in their attempts to find work and their wives struggled to put a decent meal on the table.

Shopping spree

Right: The Kings Head Buildings were erected on Cloth Hall Street in 1924, just over 30 years before this picture of the arcade and George Hall's store was taken. Hall's advertised that it was ' a house of quality and keen values'. Some readers might recall coming here to get kitted out for school. There were grey shirts, ties, blazers, trousers, pleated skirts and those appalling PE knickers that every girl dreaded wearing. It must have been about late February or early March as the left hand window had a poster proclaiming 'Easter wedding gifts'. Quite what was different about a present for a bride and groom from March to October is a mystery, but Hall's obviously thought that the sign would attract custom. It was a popular time for weddings. Couples who tied the knot just before the start of the new financial year in April could claim the married allowance for all the previous tax year, so it was worth a good bit of cash to seize this opportunity. After all, it was not often that you could get something out

of the treasury for nothing. A June bride was a pretty thought, but pragmatic couples, especially Yorkshire ones who knew the value of hard brass, opted for the back end of March instead and said 'thanks' to Macmillan or whoever was Chancellor of the Exchequer at the time.

Bottom left: Victoria Lane is now often used as a pedestrianised cut through between Boot's and River Island from Kings Street to the library. In 1958 it had its own collection of little shops that were fronted by a cobbled roadway. Lipton's Ceylon tea was heavily advertised at the corner shop and this was during the days when coffee drinking was mainly for those who lived behind chintz curtains and had bay windows to the front room. Lipton's tea is one of the most famous of all the names linked with this beverage. It fell under the Unilever banner in 1973. The history of tea drinking is lost in antiquity, though it is widely thought to have originated in China's Yangtze valley around 350BC, before cultivation spread into Japan. However, tea drinking is not recorded in Europe until the 16th century and only introduced into Britain when first publicly sold at Garway's Coffee House in London in 1657. During the late 17th and 18th centuries, the East India Company played a major role in popularising the beverage and in an effort to perpetuate this monopoly, encouraged the government to pass the Tea Act of 1773 that precipitated the Boston Tea Party. In later years, British planters made large fortunes in Ceylon (Sri Lanka) and India, similar to the profits made by sugar plantation owners in Jamaica.

Below: The Devonshire Buildings, on the corner of Victoria Lane and King Street, have now been replaced by a rather plain and uninspiring construction, though it is still home to Boot's. No one ever meets at Boot's corner any more, as this spot used to be known. Back in 1950, when this view was captured, it was a popular place for sweethearts to meet up before going off to the Ritz, Tudor or Curzon cinemas. At this time there were about two dozen picture houses in the town, such was the popularity of a night out at 'the flicks'. Young men probably got their Saturday night suit at Burton's, the 'tailor of taste', seen to the right, while their girlfriends were well pleased with the lipstick and face powder they got from the company that first saw the light of day in Nottingham. Jesse Boot, later Lord Trent, opened the first of his many shops there in 1877. His father had an interest, that Jesse inherited, in country potions and remedies. He experimented with all manner of combinations of herbs that he turned into patent medicines. Boot's shops, though, concentrated on more established lines as Jesse opened other stores in Lincoln, Sheffield and Derby. He became well loved for his charity work, giving away much of his fortune. He died in 1931, by which time his name had appeared on every high street up and down the land.

Above: Women did the shopping in November 1952. A group of them was obviously taken by something it had spotted in John Hawkins' window at 26 New Street. The ladies were well wrapped up against the autumnal chill, with coats that were cut to hang down to mid calf length, in keeping with the fashion of the day. Most of those we can see carried large handbags or shopping bags and many wore hats or headscarves. It was still uncommon to see a bareheaded woman out and about in town and you certainly never saw one doing anything so shocking as smoking a cigarette in public. The Fifty Shilling Tailor was an establishment patronised by their husbands. Henry Price (1877-1963) was a Leeds man. He recognised that, despite money being tight in the interwar years, men still wanted to dress as elegantly as they could afford. He spotted a niche in the market and established his chain, selling cheap, but acceptable, clothing. Soon he had a string of stores across the country that remained popular throughout the 1950s until greater prosperity and a desire for more fashionable clothing altered purchasing patterns. Price was knighted in 1937 and, after his passing, left a legacy of fond memories of the days when his suits cost just £2.50, in today's terminology.

Top right: Looking from Market Place over the junction of Kirkgate with Westgate, John William Street comes into view. Its corners are now dominated by McDonald's on the right and Frankie and Benny's eating place on the opposite side. The site of latter establishment, and several of its neighbouring retail outlets, was once occupied by Rushworth's department store. For much of the last century most towns had their own examples of such longstanding family businesses, but so many went to the wall as shopping fads changed during the latter third of the 1900s and large chain stores bought out the minnows.

Rushworth's was founded in 1875. Pictured here in 1953, it had still to acquire the double faced electric clock, the first of its kind in this country, that was installed above the store in 1960. Its three foot dial and continuous revolution was quite a talking point, but not for long as the business closed towards the end of that decade that brought us the mini skirt and the Beatles. But, the focus of attention was not on fashion or music in this view. The forthcoming coronation of Queen Elizabeth II on 2 June was uppermost in everyone's minds, as the large banner and decorations demonstrate. Street parties and joyous celebrations abounded as everyone, quite literally, waved the flag.

Right: The Meltham branch of the Co-op was having a week promoting Heinz baby foods on 25 February 1952. Farley's rusks and thick, syrupy orange juice supplemented infants' diets in those early NHS days and those of us now in our 50s have fond memories of the toddler treats that we enjoyed. Clinics encouraged young mothers to search out nutritious foods for their little ones in an era when some rationing was still with

us. The Heinz company was one of the first to offer a form of convenience food for the young and busy mums were only too happy to take the products on board. They needed opportunities to cut a few corners as labour saving devices were few and far between. They were, in the main, washing nappies and cleaning the house without electric appliances and any assistance in easing the burden of running the home and bringing up the children was very welcome.

Henry John Heinz (1844-1919) showed entrepreneurial flair from an early age, and was selling vegetables from the family garden to neighbours and grocers by the age of 12. In 1869 Henry went into business with L Clarence Noble as Heinz & Noble, their first product being horseradish sauce. In 1886 Heinz travelled to London and began distributing his goods through Fortnum and Mason, establishing the international nature of the company that he had set up with his cousin in 1876 after the original enterprise with Noble had folded.

Below: In the autumn of 1958, Timothy White's and Taylor's was one of Boot's greatest rivals in the field of dispensing chemists. Its main store in Huddersfield stood on the corner of Queen Street and King Street. The view down Queen Street looked towards St Paul's and to where that part of the ring road known as Queensgate now runs. We are now dwarfed by the Kingsgate shopping centre to the left and along, from where the wallpaper shop once stood. Somehow or other, the chemist's building has survived, though former occupants have long disappeared. The Sony Centre Galleria is in its stead and, as a further sign of the technological times, Jessop's and its digital photography services can be found where Buzzy B stores used to trade. Timothy White's was more than just a chemist's shop as it was somewhere that little boys could go in search of a birthday present for mum. A ten year old's imagination was fairly restricted when it came to shopping for female relatives, but the chemist's goods were a safe bet. A little presentation box of bath salts, talcum powder and toilet water was just the job. When the lad's mother accepted the gift she smiled sweetly and ruffled his hair. She then popped the gift in her dressing table drawer alongside the similar sets he bought for her last year and at Christmas as well.

Above: In 1958, Hilton's footwear shop was on the corner of King Street and Cross Church Street, opposite George Hutchison's shop. The latter dealt in toys, games, fancy goods and bankrupt stock. A ladies' hair stylist's was located above Hutchison's, boasting the fanciful name of Maison Terry. Presumably, this was meant to encourage women to consider the establishment as chic and continental in flavour. Half a century ago, it was just men's or women's hairdressers. There was no such thing as unisex. The male of the species opted for a straightforward barber who dealt in the traditional short back and sides. Some of the younger element, though, had their own ideas and demanded square necks or DA styles at the back. Sideburns were often grown down to the ear lobe and quaffed fronts swept back and kept in place by a healthy dob of Brylcreem. At Maison Terry, mature women settled for a perm or colour rinse, though some of their daughters abandoned the Toni for a peroxide bottle to look like Marilyn Monroe. Schofield's wallpaper shop could easily satisfy most decorating needs because customers had little artistic adventure in those days. A paper with a floral pattern would do very nicely and magnolia paint instead of brown was about as adventurous as they got.

This part of Buxton Road, or New Street as it became, was crammed with shoe or clothes shops vying for our custom. Dunn's and Etam catered for men's and women's fashions, respectively, while True Form and Stylo made sure that we were well shod. The retail giant, Marks and Spencer, despite its recent trials and tribulations, still flourishes on this same spot. Alongside it, the entrance to Market Avenue can be seen. Always an area for quirky shops, it still has a number of specialists, trading in such varied commodities as Belgian chocolates, collectable teddies, skateboards and out of the ordinary gifts. New Street is now pedestrianised from Cloth Hall Street to the ring road but, nearly half a century ago, lorries and wagons, even those drawn by horses if the road sign is to be believed, trundled along here. This was an era when the country was really feeling as if it had turned the postwar corner. The austerity years of the 1940s and early 1950s began to fall away into the past as employment boomed, pay packets bulged and rationing became a memory. The Prime Minister of the day, Harold Macmillan, christened Supermac' by cartoonists, told us that 'We have never had it so good' in a speech he made in July the previous year. The jangling tills of high street shopkeepers and motor showroom proprietors bore testament that Britain was back on its feet again.

Above: This stretch of New Street shows the portion from Market Place to King Street. Pictured at the start of the swinging 60s, new shop fronts sat uneasily beneath the smoke blackened architecture of yesteryear. It was just after two in the afternoon, according to the clock above W Greenwood's jewellers, but shopping activity seemed to be quite light. A large advertising sign for Wills' Capstan cigarettes hung above the corner building, reminding us that the perils of tobacco were not fully appreciated by the general public at the start of the decade that saw the emergence of a youth culture that helped change the face of retailing. In 1960, most children were expected to follow in the paths of their parents in education, fashion and morals. But, the purchasing power of the ever more affluent youth had an effect that ushered in change. Boutiques and trendy clothes shops forced many a traditional outfitter out of business and shops selling sheet music and pianos had quickly to gear up to 45s and guitars. Barbers and hair stylists went unisex, pubs became bars and parents gritted their teeth as girls and boys spent the night together. Authority was challenged as never before as ban the bomb and bring on the pill became the mantra by which many young people started to live.

Sporting life

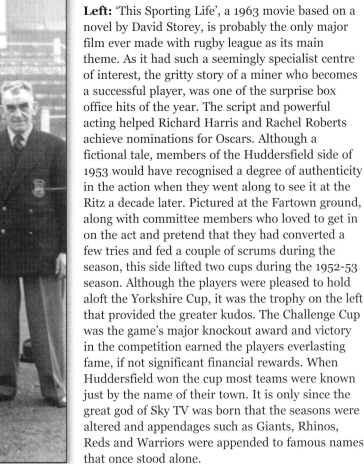

Left: 'This Sporting Life', a 1963 movie based on a novel by David Storey, is probably the only major film ever made with rugby league as its main theme. As it had such a seemingly specialist centre of interest, the gritty story of a miner who becomes a successful player, was one of the surprise box office hits of the year. The script and powerful acting helped Richard Harris and Rachel Roberts achieve nominations for Oscars. Although a fictional tale, members of the Huddersfield side of 1953 would have recognised a degree of authenticity in the action when they went along to see it at the Ritz a decade later. Pictured at the Fartown ground, along with committee members who loved to get in on the act and pretend that they had converted a few tries and fed a couple of scrums during the season, this side lifted two cups during the 1952-53 season. Although the players were pleased to hold aloft the Yorkshire Cup, it was the trophy on the left that provided the greater kudos. The Challenge Cup was the game's major knockout award and victory in the competition earned the players everlasting fame, if not significant financial rewards. When Huddersfield won the cup most teams were known just by the name of their town. It is only since the great god of Sky TV was born that the seasons were altered and appendages such as Giants, Rhinos, Reds and Warriors were appended to famous names that once stood alone.

Above: Rugby League is quintessentially a north country sport, despite many attempts to widen its appeal to the southern masses. In the 1960s, long before Grandstand was forced to commit its resources to covering such yawn inducing offerings as rowing, synchronised swimming and rhythmic gymnastics, the BBC budget permitted its outside broadcast cameras to bring us the winter excitement of motorcycle scrambling, rallying and rugby league. Armchair spectators became hooked on the oval ball game, mainly thanks to the idiosyncratic commentaries of Eddie Waring. His 'oop and unders' and 'early baths' became part of the folklore at a time when there were real characters about, including not only players and pundits, but referees like 'Sergeant Major' Clay as well. Sadly, most of those couch potatoes in the south stayed firmly put and only London Broncos have ever claimed any form of real standing in the south. Before the days of television coverage, Huddersfield was a major force in the game. One of its great periods was in the immediate postwar era. The 1948-49 side won the championship play off at Maine Road, Manchester City's former soccer ground. The game was played on 14 May 1949 in front of a record 75,194 spectators who were thrilled by the narrow 13-12 victory over 'The Wires' of Warrington.

Above: One of the greatest names in football is seen here in the dark strip, playing for Leeds United, as he anxiously watches his goalkeeper, Scott, safely take a cross from the wing at Leeds Road on 23 August 1952. John Charles was known as the 'gentle giant' because, despite his massive frame, he played the game fairly and honestly. He began his career with Swansea City before moving to Leeds in 1948. He was equally adept in the centre of the defence as up front and his all round talents came to the notice of Italy's mighty Juventus, to whom he was transferred for a then massive £65,000 in 1957. He was revered there in a way few foreign players have ever been. Despite their respect for visiting talent, home fans were more concerned with their own stars. Jimmy Glazzard, seen here moving in ready to pounce on any mistake, was one of the names the old timers amongst us will fondly remember. He was signed from Altofts Colliery, near Wakefield, in October 1943 and continued working as a miner during the 1940s. On occasions he would work a shift and then travel in with the fans before donning his kit for a three o'clock kick off! A prolific centre forward, he was instrumental in Town's promotion run during this season and scored the only goal of the game against Leeds in front of 35,230 fans.

Right: Huddersfield Town holds a number of records, the most notable of which being the hat trick of Division One championships in the mid 1920s. Another less glorious one is centred on a particular match played on 21 December 1957. Diehard supporters made the long, arduous journey south in days before motorways were heard of to follow their side on its last away game before Christmas. Charlton Athletic and the Valley played host to our boys and the home terraces were silenced early in the game as Town ran up a seemingly invincible 5-1 lead with less than half an hour to play. Visiting fans could hardly conceal their merriment as their boys in blue and white

ran riot. Those smiles receded a little when Charlton pulled one back and then another and yet another. They disappeared completely when, not only was an equaliser scored, but Athletic actually turned things around completely to take the lead 6-5. Shell-shocked Town managed to grab an equaliser, but with only two minutes to go, Charlton completed the most amazing comeback anyone on the ground had ever seen to win 7-6. Never before or since has a side knocked in six goals in a League match and come away pointless. Conwell and Taylor, the beleaguered Huddersfield defenders, could only watch as Leary powered in his header.

Top right: 'On me ead', son!' You can almost hear the words shouting out from the photograph as Town's Dick Krzywicki ran into penalty box in the sixth minute of the home game against Watford on the last day of the 1969-70 season. He timed his move perfectly, getting in between several defenders, including Garvey (4) and Eddy (6), to glance the cross beyond goalkeeper Walker into the far corner of the net. Krzywicki was more of a flying winger than a prolific goalscorer, but he made his mark on this game in the latter role. He scored twice in the 3-1 victory that saw the blue and whites lift the Second Division trophy, ensuring that the 28,000 crowd could welcome a

return to the top flight at the start of the next season. Dick Krzywicki, as well as being a good footballer with a memorable, if unspellable name, became part of soccer trivia in the 1970s. He was one quarter of the answer of a much asked quiz question - 'Name an Englishman, Irishman, Scotsman and Welshman from the Football League whose names end with the letter 'i' and have all played international soccer.' The solution to the conundrum is Bonetti (Chelsea), Mancini (Arsenal), Macari (Manchester United) and our very own tricky Dickie. His sporting connection with the area lives on in his son, Nick, who is the professional at Elland Golf Club.

Right: Huddersfield Town was one of the glamour clubs of the 1920s. It was as powerful as the likes of Chelsea and Manchester United today. The club entered the Football League in 1910 and, despite the interruptions naturally caused by World War I, continued to develop as a force to be feared by longer established sides. Its first piece of major silverware was secured in 1922 at Stamford Bridge in the last FA Cup Final before Wembley Stadium became the venue. 'Proud' Preston was overcome 1-0 and Town was now proven to be a team to be respected. The Division One title was won in 1923-24 and, not content with this success, Huddersfield Town retained the championship for a further two seasons, becoming the first side to win a hat trick of titles. Quite remarkably, manager Herbert Chapman went on to repeat this feat with Arsenal. However, despite continuing to be a top outfit in the 1930s, the postwar period saw the Leeds Road boys struggle to

keep up with the 'big boys' Much of the 1950s and 1960s were spent in the second division, but the influence of several former Manchester United players helped the side return to the top flight. With Ian Greaves as manager, Henry Cockburn the coach and Jimmy Nicholson (holding the trophy) as captain, Town ended 1969-70 as champions of Division Two.

Bottom left: But for the netting and the pitch markings, this could almost be a scene from the game played with an oval ball as it seems a successful tackle has just been made or a winning try scored. However, this was still a celebratory occasion for Huddersfield Town soccer club. Ian Robins, seen crashing to the ground in a cloud of dust, had just stuck his head in amongst the flying boots to score the club's 100th league goal of the season. Robins scored again to help secure the 2-1 victory over Hartlepool United on 3 May 1980 that meant that we had won the Division Four title. Although the 16,807 fans on the terraces celebrated the success, the level to which Town had sunk during the 1970s was cause for grave concern. At the start of the decade the club played host to Liverpool, Leeds, Arsenal, Spurs and all the other great names in English soccer. By early 1978 the once formidable pride of Yorkshire was languishing close to the foot of the league's basement division, with one eye on the very bottom rung that would have meant applying for re-election and risking banishment to non league soccer. Fortunately, an unheralded member of the coaching staff was appointed as manager when the club was at its lowest ebb. Mick Buxton turned things around and guided Town to two promotions in the early 1980s up into Division Two.

Below: Manager Ian Greaves served our soccer club faithfully for six years. Football management is one of those jobs from which you seldom retire. A person is either sacked or jumps ship before being pushed overboard. The most chilling words that can ever be heard in this environment come when the chairman of the club states publicly, 'We have every confidence in the manager'. It is then obvious to everyone that it is time to look elsewhere as the axe is about to fall. Brian Clough, that doughty old warhorse who found great success at Derby County and Notts Forest, summed it up in one of his books. He entitled one chapter 'What directors know about football' and left it as one blank page! Greaves was appointed as manager of Huddersfield Town in June 1968, just over a fortnight after his 36th birthday. Despite his comparative youth, he had a fine pedigree, being a former Busby Babe and well schooled in the art of attractive football that saw his former club lift the European Cup a couple of weeks before his arrival at Leeds Road. Following just two years in charge, Greaves had guided Town back into Division One. Here he is seated in the middle of the side that opened the 1971-72 campaign. It was to be the last season we would have at the top level and, in 1974, we were relegated into the third division. Greaves resigned his post before the chairman had an opportunity to offer his support.

Back row: C Dobson, T Poole, G Pierce, D Lawson, M Barry
Middle Row: J Nicholson, T Cherry, D Clarke, B Mahoney, R Ellam, T Dolan, R Krzywicki
Front row: J McGill, J Lawson, R Hoy, F Worthington, I Greaves, S Smith, G Hutt, A Jones, L Chapman

Working life

This scene from 4 May 1950, with its old lorries and trucks that you would just love to own as Dinky toys in order to preserve them, shows Brown and Cheetham's garage and showroom on Leeds Road. The hand-cranked Cleveland petrol pumps are also a period piece, as was the service provided by the attendant. A car arrived at the garage and the driver was assured of personal attention as the filler cap was unscrewed and fuel dispensed into the tank. The windscreen received a quick wipeover and engine oil levels regularly checked. Payment was offered and change given, all without the driver leaving the sanctuary of his seat. The Brown and Cheetham garage was an agent for Morris cars.

The company was founded by William Morris (1877-1963). Son of a farm labourer, he rose from humble beginnings to be made Viscount Nuffield in 1938. By then he had moved through the business ranks of cycle repairs, cycle and motorcycle manufacture to establishing his motorcar company at Cowley in 1913. As his marriage was childless, he had no issue to whom he could pass on his fortune, so he turned his attention to using his wealth to help others. His philanthropic activities began in the early 1930s and beneficiaries including the Nuffield Institute for Medical Research, the University of Oxford, the Nuffield Trust, Nuffield College, Oxford and the Nuffield Foundation.

Above: This was a publicity photograph for Daz, the washing powder that is still a top seller today. Taken on 19 November 1952, it attracted the attention of housewives who were desperate to find anything that would alleviate the blues of Monday's washing day. Reddened hands were the order of the day, as women battled with dolly tubs and mangles. The electric washing machine was but a pipedream for most as they sweated over the washing mountain created by the family's dirty clothing from the previous seven days. The level of grime was much higher than it is today. Chimneys in factories and on homes belched out smoke from coal fired furnaces and grates, covering our industrial heartland in a layer of soot that soiled clothes from the minute they were donned. No wonder our mums and wives turned to anything that would help just a little bit. Unilever versus Procter and Gamble was the major bout in the marketing fight for housewives' custom in soap powders. Persil and Rinso did battle against Tide and Oxydol, with honours being about even. In 1952, Unilever launched Surf, but Procter and Gamble hit back with Daz, a blue powder containing a chemical bleach and intended for the 'boiling' wash. The company was impressed by the extent to which the British housewife boiled clothes and hoped that Daz would capture some of the Persil market. Unilever replied by producing a synthetic 'boiling' powder, Omo, also coloured blue, in 1954.

Three years after Sainsbury's opened its first self service store in Croydon, Jubb's grocers followed suit. The firm's head office was at Serpentine Road, Cleckheaton and this photograph from 12 November 1953 shows its outlet at 13-15 Broad Lane, Moldgreen. Change was on hand for local shoppers used to ordering their fresh and packaged food over the counter. Shiny new display cabinets groaned under the weight of goods that housewives now had to carry for themselves to the checkout till. The personal relationship between shopkeeper and customer was about to be consigned to the shelves of history. Where once a man in a striped apron knew how thickly Mrs Higginbottom liked her bacon slicing, now there was just a pile of regular cuts from which she had to choose herself. The van at the door, laden with outsize advertorial packets of washing powder, porridge and cheese wedges, was as bright and new as the shop interior, but not everyone blessed the move. The grocer's delivery boy was out of work. No longer did a shopper select her items with the man behind the counter and have the purchases made up into an order box for the lad to bring round to her door on the front of his bike. She now had to pester hubby to get his new Ford Popular off the drive and come with her to collect the week's shopping.

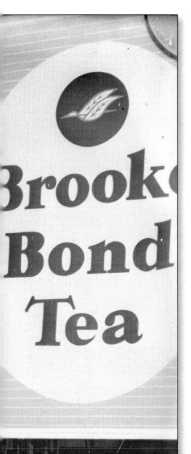

Left: They have gone from our television sets now, thanks to marketing decisions and animal rights do-gooders, but those chimps will never be forgotten. Their appearance in countless television commercials for PG tips always brought a smile to a viewer's face. Put into storylines or situations in which humans found themselves, the antics of our closest cousins were often better than some of the TV programmes they interrupted. One of the best loved scenes involved removal men/chimps and a piano. 'Do you know this piano's on my foot?' was matched by the answer, 'Just hum it and I'll accompany you.' Classic! There was no monkey business about at this 1956 exhibition stand. A free cup of Brooke Bond tea was on offer and we are sure that the girls must have dished out a few thousand cuppas during the day. The prices of the tea and the weights in which it was sold date all of us who still refer to a 50p piece as 'ten bob' or immediately convert 500 grams into 'a pound and a bit'. The bargain offers on show included a quarter pound each of PG Tips and Dividend tea, plus a bottle of Dividend Bon and a dozen boxes of matches, all for 4s 6d (22.5p) instead of the usual total cost of 6s 6d (32.5p). The inclusion of all those matches in the deal left us nonplussed, unless the shopper was expected to have trouble boiling the kettle.

Below: These mill girls, taking a moment out to pose for the camera on 11 February 1960, worked in an atmosphere far removed from the one their mothers and former generations had to experience. This part of Moxon Mill, Highburton was a long way removed from the old textile mills where the flying shuttles and clanking machinery offered a hazardous working environment. The continuous noise left many with hearing difficulties and young girls risked life and limb crawling under moving belts to free some section of the looms that had got stuck or were malfunctioning. Their days were long and the remuneration poor. Fibres drifted through the air, clogging lungs and promoting respiratory problems. Some contracted mouth cancer from the practice of wetting yarn to make it easier to fix in place. How fortunate these women were to be employed in such bright, airy conditions. By this time, though, the British textile trade was well in decline, with cheap imports from Asia having flooded the market. Every valley across Lancashire and Yorkshire once had cotton, wool and silk mills in abundance that attracted workers away from the land in the 19th century as they flooded down from the hills in search of industrialised work. By 1960, such mills were gradually being abandoned and huge numbers lay derelict.

Shaw & Hallas - Feet first

'Selling shoes that don't come back to people who do' is more than just a catchy slogan to Huddersfield's best known footwear outlet, Shaw & Hallas Ltd in Market Walk.

For the family-owned firm which has been selling, and originally making, shoes in Huddersfield since the time of the Crimean War, a commitment to quality and customer satisfaction is a business philosophy which has been passed down unchanged through many generations.

From buttoned boots to brogues, court shoes to clogs, from winklepickers and stilettos through to today's currently fashionable footwear the staff at Shaw & Hallas have seen it all.

Shaw & Hallas came into being through a combination of two small local firms whose history dates from 1864.

These days when almost all footwear is factory made it's easy to forget that before the first world war the majority of boots and shoes were made by those who sold them - and often made to measure like suits and dresses.

Today factory production has almost killed off those specialised skills, but in the 19th century shoemakers were greatly prized for their expertise, and the best were in great demand from customers who knew quality workmanship when they saw it.

Top left: *Founders of Shaw & Hallas Mr John Shaw (left) and Mr John Elliot Hallas.* ***Below:*** *John Shaw pictured in the doorway of 8 Westgate, 1889.*

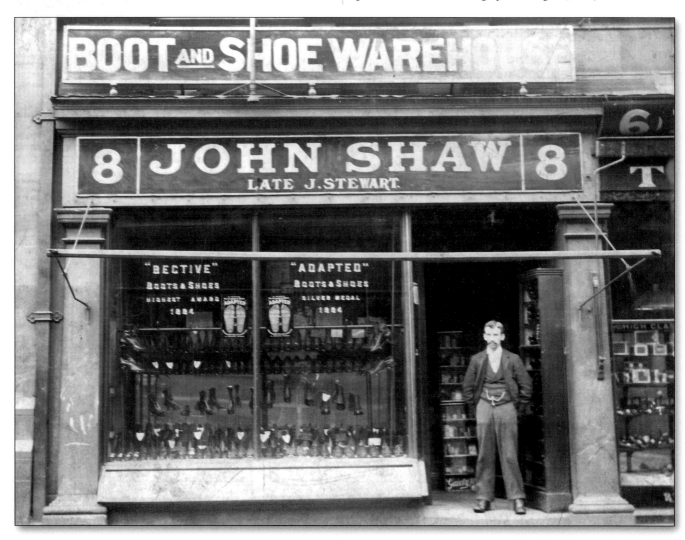

It was in 1864 that John Shaw took over the business of Dicks of 8 Westgate Huddersfield. Dicks was a gutta percha (a natural resin similar to rubber) dealer but John Shaw began to make and repair shoes; his wife Hannah, who had previously run a lace and millinery shop on Cross Church street and later in Macaulay Street, now joined him.

John and Hannah Shaw had two sons and two daughters. One daughter, Emily, married George, the son of Elliott Hallas who had a shoe shop in Holmfirth. The Hallases' shop moved to Buxton Road (subsequently New Street) and later moved to John Williams Street. That shop later became George Field's and later Rushworths' extension.

In 1914, as the opening salvoes of the first world war were heard, the Shaws and the Hallases amalgamated to form a limited company; they put a double front in their shop in Westgate, premises which would later form the lower part of Cuthberts chemists.

The change from making shoes to selling 'made up' brands had started in the early 1900s 'Bective' Brand button boots and 'K' shoes.

By then the personalities involved in the business were the founders' sons John (Jack) William Shaw and George Hallas.

In 1923 the firm moved to 10-12 John William Street, and John Douglas Shaw, grandson of one founder, joined the business. There they would remain as tenants of the YMCA until 1961.

Jack Hallas, Elliott Hallas' grandson, joined the firm after the 1939-45 war. John Michael Shaw, great grandson of John and Hannah Shaw arrived in 1958.

By then shoemaking had given way to retailing, selling the finished product, though repairing would continue until the 1980s.

Over the years leather had begun to give way to rubber and fabrics, though leather uppers and soles would continue to predominate until the 1960s. Plastic soles have since come to be the most common, Shaw & Hallas however, has always believed in the comfort and health benefits of leather and still stock plenty of leather-soled shoes for men, whilst most ladies' and children's shoes still feature leather uppers.

The YMCA building was purchased for redevelopment in 1961 and the firm moved to 28 Market Street, whilst also opening a children's shop at 7 New North Road and a salon at 48 New North Road. Both New North Road premises would later close due to subsequent redevelopment. The salon, incidentally, was on the premises of the old Huddersfield College of Music where many notable musicians received their training.

In 1968 the Shaw family acquired the whole of the shares in the company, but kept the name of Shaw & Hallas.

Top: The first Shaw & Hallas shop after amalgamation in 1914.

Following the compulsory purchase of the salon for road building by Huddersfield Corporation in 1970 the company decided to expand by opening an outlet in another town. Luckily suitable shop premises became available in Cross Street, Manchester and a new company was formed to develop this: Marrum, Shaw & Co Ltd, an association between Shaw & Hallas and the German manufacturing house, 'Salamander', of Kornwestheim. The new shop would be a happy combination of Shaw & Hallas management and a ready availability of continental merchandise.

The Manchester shop opened in October 1970, serving a large city with fashion shoes and leather clothes whilst giving full personal attention in the well established tradition of Shaw & Hallas. Other ventures would subsequently be launched in Bradford and Dewsbury before the firm consolidated once again, centralising its business in Huddersfield.

Meanwhile back in Huddersfield a new additional Shaw & Hallas shoe shop would open in the Pack Horse Walk development in 1972, a branch which would operate there until 1977.

By then the Chairman of the still independently owned family firm was John D Shaw, well known as a Mason, Rotarian, YMCA worker and golfer. John Shaw had by then being fitting shoes to feet for half a century and during that period had been active through the Chamber of Trade and Shoemen's organisations to improve standards throughout retailing.

Managing Director was by then John Michael Shaw the fourth generation of the family. Originally Michael had trained as a rose grower but he returned to Huddersfield to carry on the family business. Also involved in the YMCA, golf and local trader work Michael had been Chairman of the National Shoe Retailers Council in the North East region and National President of the IFRA (Independent Footwear Retailers Association).

By the late 1980s Michael had been joined in the business by his daughter Vicky Shaw (Later Vicky Devlin). The firm moved from its Market Street premises in 1994.

Top: Inside The Salon on New North Road in the 1960s.
Above: Mr John Michael Shaw fitting a customer in the Market Street shop, early 1970s.

Today the business is run by Vicky Devlin, trading in Huddersfield's Market Walk and at Springfield Mill Denby Dale.

Though shoes are no longer made by the firm, and though there are now few British shoe manufacturers left, the Shaw & Hallas commitment to quality remains. Top quality fashionable and traditional footwear is now sourced not only from Britain but also from Germany, France, Spain, Portugal and Italy.

Vicky Devlin has revolutionised the control of the buying and selling of shoes, introducing computerised systems without which businesses today would soon fall behind their competitors. Yet the firm remains committed to remaining small, a policy which enables it to keep everything personal - something which no large chain can ever hope to achieve.

During the history of the firm a policy of personal service has been consistently pursued, and this continues to this

day: the company has matched this with merchandise of high quality. Despite the many changes the demand for quality remains the same.

The firm has constantly kept up with customers demands for increasing quality as affluence has increased down the decades; fashion and comfort may be often paramount durability is a hidden quality which is only noticed when it is absent.

Though Shaw & Hallas may be based in Huddersfield customers travel from far and wide to seek out specialist products like narrow and wide fittings, real fitting skill, superior quality and a personal service.

And what's the secret of keeping a business running effectively for more than a century and half?

There certainly have been hurdles to overcome down the years; each generation has faced its own crises: two world wars, inflation in the 1970s, taxes, red tape, the loss of company records in a fire at the firm's office in St George's Square, increasing local and national government legislation - and now European directives.

But according to Vicky there are no secrets to survival - just the family's determination to persist. That persistence involves long hours, hard physical and mental work, and often not a little worry. The result is not only the means to earn a living but also the satisfaction of a job well done to the best of their ability, a happy family of workers and the smiles, even broad grins, on the faces of satisfied customers.

Top: Mrs Emily Shaw and son Mr John Michael Shaw.
Above right: Vicky Devlin, daughter of John Michael Shaw, Managing Director of Shaw & Hallas. Right: Today's shop on Market Walk, home to Shaw & Hallas since 1994.

W T Johnson - Finishing the job

WT Johnson & Sons Ltd, the Huddersfield company producing world-class finishes for woollen and worsted cloth, was founded in 1916 when Walter Thomas Johnson set up in business in premises on Wakefield Road. He had decided to take the brave step of branching out with his own company, aged about 50 years, after serving as Foreman Finisher at Glendinning's. He took his son, Walter Marshall Johnson ('WM'), into partnership with him; this was a complete change of direction for the younger Walter who had only recently passed his Civil Service exams. Today Walter Thomas's great-grandsons are continuing the family tradition, the fourth generation to be involved in the business.

The two Walters, father and son, worked together for the first few years, but later Walter senior's other sons, Tom and Frank, joined them, and the tradition that all family members would be fully acquainted with each and every part of the business began. Although over the years some Johnsons have inevitably spent more time on one area than another, they are all conversant with the technical side of things and endeavour to keep abreast of what is happening in the workshop and with their customers.

Many difficulties had to be overcome down the years. One of the first hurdles to be surmounted by the infant Johnson firm was to repay a personal loan granted by a Mr Sykes of Norwood Green. He is also believed to have owned the premises occupied by the firm. Today the firm is still operating from the same address in Wakefield Road, Huddersfield but the site has seen significant expansion and development over the years. Much of this development took place in the 1950s when land adjacent to the site which had previously been Hudder-sfield Corporation allotments was acquired for new building work - indeed they would have liked more, but this was not made available to the company.

In the 18th and 19th centuries, in the early days of the Colne Valley's woollen industry, work was carried out by firms which did everything, starting with the raw wool from the sheep, through spinning, weaving, dyeing and finishing. As time went on, however, some firms started to specialise on one process, Johnsons was one of them, (though in the 1970s Johnsons took over Tom Lees & Co, Dyers from Honley, renaming the company DP Dyers Ltd). Concentrating on a specific area gave a number of advantages - they were able to build up expertise in that particular process and were able to direct their resources into the best available machinery for the job. Some like Crowther's continued to offer the entire range, but they were in the minority.

Johnson's chose to specialise in finishing, and invested accordingly. Though the equipment available for

Above and below: Early machine used by WT Johnson. Right: Early quality procedures, which would include burling and mending, the art of finding slubs in material and removing them.

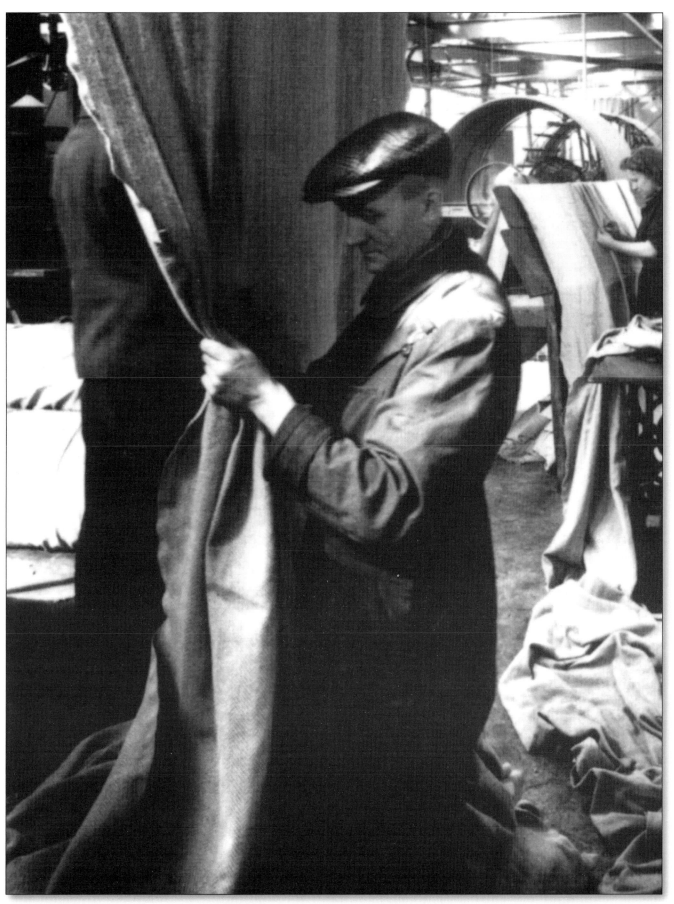

carrying out the finishing process has changed over time as technology has brought new levels of accuracy and complexity to the procedure, the original raison d'etre of the company remains the same as it was during World War I, namely to take woollen cloth as it comes straight from the loom and wash it (usually with soap and water), dry it and press it using the most up-to-date machinery. A great number of variations are now possible in each of these three stages of the finishing process. This enables Johnson's to add real value to the fabric it finishes and become an important contributor to the creation of new fabrics. The quality and uniformity of the finish is also of paramount importance. Today's customers demand repeatable finishes due to the popularity of 'mix and match' clothing - items of an outfit bought separately need to look good together and be a genuine match.

To remain in business all companies need to stay ahead of their competitors, and this is particularly so when the industry concerned is in decline, as is the case with the woollen industry. Many mills in the West Riding which used to resound to the roar of busy weaving looms are now derelict, and it is a testament to the quality of the Johnson treatments that the company is still in business in this highly competitive international market. It is not only local firms which represent rival bidders for available work but also developing countries which have significantly lower labour costs as well as Italian companies nearer home which specialise in the same field.

Today the company employs over 90 people, and takes pride in providing a product which it believes is the best in the business - a result of nearly a century of Johnson expertise and consistently investing in the best staff and equipment available.

Meanwhile no-one has ever been able to explain satisfactorily exactly why in the 17th century the wool trade suddenly began to dominate this area. England had already had a thriving woollen industry for centuries, but that industry was based in Yorkshire's East Riding, East Anglia and Somerset. So important had the wool trade already been to the national economy that even today the Lord Chancellor still sits on the 'Woolsack' in the House of Lords.

There were no new technical innovations at the time which might explain the phenomenal growth of weaving in the West Riding of Yorkshire. Some suggest that it was demand for cloth to make uniforms for the armies then fighting all over Europe which stimulated new demands on British weavers.

Others suggest that the enclosure of common land drove local smallholders to find something else to do with their idle hands. Still others point to the trade guilds, early trade unions, which in other parts of the country restricted recruitment to the weaving trade even in the face of vastly increased demand. These ancient institutions did not

company to supply it, therefore minimising costs and, secondly, the water would be pure, making it ideal for washing the fabric. The Manchester firm of drilling experts, Thomas Matthews, was consulted and having studied geological maps of the area felt sure that water would he found on the site and agreed to find it. Boring commenced in the late 1930s and the hole reached the depth of about 300 feet which was the standard well depth, but there was no water. Undaunted, Matthews kept drilling (and invoicing Johnsons accordingly). When the hole had reached a depth of 1000 feet, 'WT' felt that further expenditure could not be justified on what seemed to be a fruitless project and called the drilling off. However Rex Matthews, who was supervising the operation, was so unshakeably convinced that water would be found that he said he would go on drilling and allow 'WT' to pay him back when he could - thus the Johnson firm received another huge benefit from a patient benefactor. Rex's confidence was not misplaced and water was indeed struck - at a depth of more than 1,500 feet (it is believed to be the deepest well in Yorkshire). The firm has reaped the benefit of its own uncontaminated free water supply since 1940 when the associated pipework was laid down.

operate strongly in the Pennine valleys, so allowing the trade to grow here at a dramatic pace.

These provided the motive and the opportunity: the means were wool and water.

Sheep there were aplenty - though not so many that they could keep up with local weavers. By the 18th century raw wool was being imported into the Colne Valley from far and wide to keep up with its looms.

One of the most important elements in the success of the Yorkshire woollen industry however has been the soft West Yorkshire water.

Water flowing down steep valleys or kept back in mill ponds could be used to drive power looms. But equally importantly the soft water made it easy to wash wool and finish cloth - a critical part of the whole process.

WT Johnson thought it would be a great advantage to have its own water supply on site brought directly from a well, for two reasons: firstly it would not have to pay the water

It is a point of pride in the company that it is a supplier of a process which meets important 'green' criteria: no detergents or synthetic additives are used in the processes and this gives the company a leading edge in today's marketing climate where 'natural' and 'sustainable' are coveted accolades. WT Johnson & Sons remains confident in its continuing ability to stay ahead of the competition, not just in its commitment to technology and profitability but also in its environmental credentials.

*Left and above: Views of WT Johnson's Mold Green premises. **Right:** The Johnson family pictured in 2000.*

Myers - An impressive mix

On the face of it, apart from being two of the area's most prominent landmarks, Emley Moor Mast and Scammonden Bridge have little in common. But there is an important link between the two: Huddersfield's Myers Group of companies, the concrete to quarrying consortium, which today has an annual turnover of £40 million and which has for decades been involved in almost every major building project in and around Huddersfield and our region - not least at Emley Moor and Scammonden.

The Myers Group based in Leeds Road, of which Johnsons Wellfield Quarries and Naylor Myers are part, was born from an idea of Jack D Myers in the late 1950s as a natural development of the family civil engineering business. The business was first incorporated in 1923 as Isaac Timmins Ltd, and which remains the parent company of the whole Myers Group.

Hervey Myers, grandfather of the current family directors, was a house builder from Mirfield. Most of his work was in the Dalton and Almondbury areas of Huddersfield building terraced and semi-detached properties. He also owned the Jesse Medley brickworks which were situated on Kilner Bank. Hervey however sold the brickworks to Elliots around 1940. In recent years the old Kilner Bank site has been landfilled and restored.

Though Hervey was already established as a builder in his own right Isaac Timmins was even better known. When Hervey acquired the Isaac Timmins business he chose to trade under the better known name.

In the early days the business was based in Firth Street but around 1930 moved to Greenhead Avenue in Dalton.

Though today the Group has around 400 employees on the payroll the business was much smaller in the early days. At the time Hervey passed the firm to his only son Jack Douglas Myers in the early 1940s there were only some 30 or so employees.

It says much for Hervey Myers that he was able to achieve so much in a period of time which is still recalled by those who lived through it as the 'Hungry Thirties'. Unemployment was rife and work of any kind hard to come by. Economic depression fed on itself: the less money folk had the less they spent, the less they spent the fewer jobs they created. Every industry was in the doldrums not least the building trade. There was however, just enough activity to keep some firms going - and Hervey Myers was determined to ensure that his would be one of them, and that he would be able to one day pass on a thriving business to his son.

The end of the great depression came in 1939, though not in a way anyone would have wished for. In September 1939 Britain declared war on Germany after Adolph Hitler had refused to withdraw his invading army from Poland. Massive government spending on armaments and fortifications now bump-started the stagnant economy. New factories were demanded, coastal defences and army camps were ordered to

Top left: Jack Myers, founder of the Myers Group.
Below: Driver Jim Throsstle about to embark with another load of readymix concrete in January 1960.

be constructed. Words like 'overtime' were heard for the first time in a generation.

The outbreak of the second world war in 1939 and the change it created in the construction market set the scene for the hand-over from Hervey to Jack Myers and a move from house building to infrastructure work. Jack had expected to be called up to serve in the armed forces but failed his medical following which he was placed in a reserved occupation, spending the war years contributing to the war effort building aerodrome facilities such as runways and air defences in the East Riding and north Lincolnshire. Most of those airbases have now disappeared and been forgotten. Between 1939 and 1945 however, those British and American airbases formed the launch pad for the thousands of bombers and fighter planes which not only defended Britain's skies from Reichmarshal Herman Goering's much-vaunted Luftwaffe, but in due course took the fight to the skies over Germany itself as the tide of war finally swung in Britain and her allies' favour.

His experiences working on large building projects would serve Jack Myers well when he returned to civilian work back in Huddersfield and the surrounding area after the end of the war.

In the post-war years civil engineering, roads and sewers became a mainstay of the business, working on district council projects in places such as Meltham, Kirkburton, Honley and Holmfirth.

In the late 1950s more ambitious projects were embarked upon for larger local authorities, working on larger road and sewer schemes for Huddersfield and Dewsbury Councils.

Though the end of the first world war a generation earlier had been followed by an economic slump the period after the second world war was unexpectedly one of continuing growth and optimism. Some parts of Britain had suffered enormous damage from German bombing, as a consequence a huge amount of building work need to be done. A vast house building programme was promised by the Government and new roads, 'motorways' they were to be called, were to be built criss-crossing the country.

Britain was about to become one enormous building site.

Jack Myers recognised there would be a need for a specialised supplier of ready mixed concrete and jointly established Readymix Huddersfield Ltd in 1959. The company which now supplies concrete from its various location around West and North Yorkshire from Penistone in the south to Skipton in the north.

Above: Laying bases for the Leeds Road Readymix Plant, 1961.

The joint venture with Naylor the pipemakers of Denby Dale to produce Readymixed concrete led to plants being established in Huddersfield and Brighouse with a site plant later established on the M62 Pennine Contract for McAlpine. The M62 site plant would be subsequently transferred to Penistone.

Mobile Concrete Pumps was established in 1969 as one of the first concrete pumping firms to operate in the North of England. Through the company's experience and expertise it has developed and operated specialised void infilling equipment under the name of Blastmixer, complementing its concrete pumping division.

Naylor Myers Building Supplies which was formed in 1973 has ten depots and is the largest trading element within the Group.

Johnsons Wellfield Quarries at Crosland Hill was established in 1854 to satisfy the demand for building stone created by the industrial revolution. The business was acquired by the Readymix Huddersfield Group in 1979 and has continued to grow, providing the impetus to embark on ambitious and continuing expansion.

Top: *Johnsons Wellfield Quarries at Crosland Hill.*
Above: *The Readymix-Huddersfield plant pictured in 1961.*

The quarry today has become the largest dimensional sandstone quarry and masonry works in Britain. A range of the world's most technical stone working machinery and age-old skills of a team dedicated to stone masons combine to produce a quality of workmanship that will ensure Johnsons continues to carry the banner of Huddersfield's 'stone' heritage.

The early 1970s saw the Group's civil engineering activities being wound down with all efforts being concentrated on Readymix, Naylor Myers builders merchants and quarrying.

By the 1990s the business was being run entirely by the Myers family, culminating in June 1998 when Naylor interests were bought out and the Myers family achieved sole ownership and control of the Group.

Today the whole group comprises Readymix Huddersfield Ltd, Naylor Myers Ltd, Johnsons Wellfield Quarries Ltd, Mobile Concrete Pumps Ltd, Mini Mix Huddersfield Ltd and Honley Skip Hire Ltd.

The current diversity of the Group means that raw materials are obtained from many different sources. Readymix obtains its aggregates from throughout Yorkshire, north Derbyshire and Nottinghamshire with cement from Lancashire. Naylor Myers sells products manufactured throughout the United Kingdom, with an increasing amount of tools and ironwork coming from the Far East. Though Johnsons quarries its own raw materials from Crosland Hill this is supplemented from time to time with sandstones from other sources. Finished stone products are now readily available from India and China with the raw materials - blockstone - coming from as far away as Australia. Sawn stone from Crosland Hill is sold throughout the United Kingdom.

This traditionally run group of companies, now solely owned by the Myers family, is proud to be able to serve the construction industry with all its requirements. Jack Myers has been followed by his son John Myers and daughter Jackie Berry who today can look back with pride at their family's contribution to such prestigious local projects as the M62 Scammonden Bridge and dam, Kingsgate shopping centre, the Galpharm Stadium, the Emley Moor mast and Winscar reservoir. And no doubt there are many more, equally prestigious projects yet to come for the Myers' of today and tomorrow.

Below: Preliminary work on erection of a concrete shell for the new Emley Moor Mast in 1969.

Holset - Turbocharged progress

A damper was quickly designed, manufactured and tested. McLaren were impressed with the test results and an order for 50 quickly followed.

Holset Engineering became a limited company on 29 March 1952. The name derives from the family names of HOLmes and CroSET. Holset was a fully owned subsidiary of BHD Engineers Limited.

Paul Croset was Holset's first Managing Director, DM Henshaw was the Chairman. Other board members were Louis Croset (Founder and Director), FB Holmes, H Whitely and P Rushworth (Secretary).

With facilities across the world including Europe, North America, South America, China and India. Huddersfield-based Holset Engineering is the world's leading designer of turbochargers for medium and heavy duty diesel engines. Its beginnings however were modest.

From 1948 to early 1952 the Company traded as a division of W C Holmes manufacturing dampers and couplings. Premises comprised of a garage and a wooden hut. WC Holmes had become interested in the flexible couplings designed by Louis Croset in 1944. During I948, W C Holmes obtained the manufacturing rights from Louis Croset, Paul Croset was persuaded to manage this new venture. He arrived in Huddersfield on 13 December 1948.

Paul Croset had earlier tested a viscous damper manufactured in the USA by Houdaille Industries. The tests showed that the Houdaille damper had a very short life. Paul designed a new damper using different materials. A patent was taken out and the manufacture and sale of viscous dampers began.

Paul Croset heard that J & H McLaren of Leeds needed a reliable damper for their marine engine. He persuaded them to let Holset produce a prototype.

At that time the Company still operated from the garage and the wooden hut and employed just 25 staff. Turnover was £4,500 but plans were in place to expand.

In August 1953, the first manufacturing bay was completed. By now the number of employees had grown to 42 and turnover to £98,000.

Competition however had been increasing since 1951 when Joseph Lucas had been given a licence to manufacture Houdaille Dampers. Fortunately, Holset had foreseen this danger and Paul Croset took his first transatlantic flight to Buffalo, New York, USA to visit the

Top: *The wooden hut from where Paul Croset was persuaded to manage the new venture.* **Right:** *The first board members of 1952.*

President of Houdaille industries. The visit was a success, each party agreed to respect each others patents and Joseph Lucas was instructed by the Ministry of Supply to grant Holset a sub-licence for Houdaille dampers.

Holset's interest in automotive radial-flow turbochargers began early in the 1950s. A licence was offered by Eberspächer of Germany who developed the first small air-cooled turbocharger for truck applications. Holset rejected this offer.

However, Holset recognised the potential of turbochargers as a key future technology and began to research the technical and manufacturing processes of turbocharging by contacting Dr Alfred Büchi, the inventor of the first turbocharger.

By April 1954, a licence had been granted from Büchi for the manufacture and sale of exhaust gas-driven turbochargers.

Meanwhile the demand for dampers in West Germany was growing so quickly that there was no alternative but to grant a manufacturing licence to Carl Hasse & Werde of Berlin in order to meet demand.

In 1955 a licence agreement was granted with Sulzer Bros of Switzerland for the manufacture of viscous

dampers for use on their own engines in the event of Holset being unable to supply.

A second manufacturing bay was completed during 1956 to accommodate the increased damper volumes.

Initial contact had been made with Louis Schwitzer of the Schwitzer Corporation of Indianapolis, USA as early as 1952. After many negotiations, a licence agreement embracing the manufacture and sale of turbochargers and rubber dampers across Europe was signed in 1957. This agreement was a key milestone in the history of Holset taking the company firmly into the turbocharger business and making Holset the only company in the world capable of handling torsional vibration problems across the whole spectrum of internal combustion engines.

After the signing of the Schwitzer contract in 1957, extra manufacturing facilities were required. Bay 3 was primarily used for the machining assembly and testing of turbochargers. At the east end of the bay, Holset's first rubber manufacturing plant was set up for the production

Top: The first office block opened in 1954 and (inset) the aftermath of the devastation left to the building by the fire in December 1967.

of inserts for rubber dampers and silicon o ring seals for turbochargers. The rubber manufacturing plant was seen as a critical part of the business. It allowed Holset to control the specifications and the properties of the rubber to ensure that the highest quality rubber could be used on all products.

By 1959 the firm was employing 95 staff, whilst annual turnover had reached £664,000.

The first production order for rubber dampers was obtained from the British Motor Corporation in November 1959. This was quickly followed by a succession of orders from Morris, Perkins, Rover, Vauxhall, Renault, Citroen and Beruet.

In 1964 the 25,000th turbocharger was produced. In honour of the occasion the turbocharger was presented to Louis Schwitzer JR., President of the Schwitzer Corporation.

Early in the morning of 3 December 1967, a fire destroyed both the production and administrative facilities at the Tunbridge site. Key records were lost: accounts, customer orders, production control data, planning, jig and tool records and component drawings. The latest IBM 1130 computer was also destroyed.

Employees, machine tool manufacturers, sub-contractors and customers all co-ordinated to ensure that production lines were kept going and delivery dates met. From the

ashes of the fire, the Holset spirit of co-operation arose enabling the Company to survive the disaster and re-build with confidence in the future.

In the four decades since then that confidence has shown to have been more than justified, despite many changes in store.

In 1973, Hanson Trust Limited acquired the BHD Group but the following year Cummins Engine Company, USA purchased Holset from Hanson for £11 million. This was the start of Holset's worldwide expansion.

September 1978 brought the millionth turbocharger off the line and saw a turnover of £26 million.

In 1983, Holset Aftermarket was established, with its headquarters in Huddersfield. Holset Aftermarket

Top: Bays 1&2 pictured after the completion of bay 2 in 1956. Above right: Bay 3 built in 1958 and primarily used for machining assembly and testing of turbochargers.

Limited Company. HRH the Duke of Kent came to visit the Huddersfield site. Five founding members of Holset - Paul Croset, Bernard Ratcliffe, Tommy Dixon, Jeff Hall and Ron Hesselden were present to enjoy the special day.

Six months later in October 2002 at the Bonneville Salt Flats, Utah Galebanks Engineering raced a Dodge Dakota with a Holset HY55V Variable Geometry Turbocharger. They broke the land speed record for a diesel pick-up truck with an amazing speed of 222mph.

In 2003, Holset's worldwide expansion continued with the relocation to larger premises in China. 2004 saw an extension to the existing plant in India and in 2005 the announcement of a further plant in Charleston, USA.

The future has never looked so bright for Holset and their turbochargers can be found breathing life into an ever larger number of the world's diesel engines.

remanufactures and sells turbochargers and spare parts through a network of independent distributors worldwide.

An assembly plant was set up in Brazil and a new manufacturing plant was built at Charleston, South Carolina, USA during the late 1980s.

Joint ventures were established with the Tata Group of Companies in India in 1994 and in 1995 in China with Wuxi Power.

During 1996, the six millionth turbocharger rolled off the assembly line. The dampers and air compressors division of the business were sold along with the couplings division allowing Holset to solely concentrate on the turbocharger market.
Following on from this, 1997 saw the relocation of all manufacturing in the USA to two sites in Charleston and Columbus.

In 1998, a brand new state-of-the-art Technical Centre was built on St. Andrew's Road in Huddersfield and in 1999 Holset Aftermarket was relocated to the same site with new purpose built facilities.

In 1998, Paul Croset OBE retired. He was awarded the OBE for his services to engineering in 1996.

On 29 March 2002, Holset celebrated its 50th Anniversary as a

Above: Office block two constructed in 1969 enabling all administrative staff to be under one roof.
Below: Holset's Technical Centre, Huddersfield.

Trojan Plastics - Working like a Trojan

As the old adage goes, mighty oaks from acorns grow: and there's no better example of that in business than Huddersfield's Trojan Plastics Ltd. It's a business where a reputation for quality counts for a great deal - even though there is no outside sales force, today the acrylic bath and shower tray manufacturer, based in Britannia Mills in Milnsbridge, is working flat out in double shifts to meet the seemingly insatiable demand for its products. Yet the company's beginnings more than 30 years ago were very modest indeed.

Indeed not only were the early years of this company modest they were also filled with the kind of disasters which few firms could be expected to survive. That Trojan not only survived, but prospered too, is down wholly to the hard work and never say die approach of its remarkable founder.

The business was created in 1974 by James Maurice Vincent Mosley. Though having begun his working life in the early 1940s as an apprentice pattern maker and joiner on ten shillings (50p) a week he later worked for Alfred Crowthers Ltd, a plumbers merchant in Northumberland Street in Huddersfield. Later JMV Mosley became sales manager for another similar firm, Neville Lumb & Co, before becoming a partner in an unsuccessful business venture, a builders merchants in Heckmondwike.

The Heckmondwike business did not create enough profit to support two partners. Instead JMV Mosley returned to his previous employer; but despite being offered the job of sales manager again he had got the taste for being self-employed. By the early 1970s JMV Mosley had rented a railway arch in Huddersfield where he was working for himself as a builders and plumbers merchant, selling wholly to the contract plumbing trade.

Below and right: *Ramsden Mill, home of Trojan Plastics. The picture right is a reconstruction view of the Mill in the early 19th century.*

Maurice's early life as a pattern maker now came in useful since patterns had to be made for the moulds in which to vacuum-form the baths from preheated acrylic sheets.

Some 200 baths were soon being turned out each week by the fledgling Trojan business and its three staff. But life was far from easy: yet another crisis was on the way. As the firm expanded established manufacturers began to take note, cutting their own prices to undermine Trojan. The large manufacturers could do this with impunity since with the huge scale of their operations they could negotiate large discounts on the cost of acrylic 'Perspex' sheet from the sole supplier, ICI.

JMV Mosley pleaded with the management at 'Perspex' to help save his business and the jobs of his staff by offering him an equal discount to that being enjoyed by competitors. The appeals fell on deaf ears - according to ICI Trojan was simply not large enough to warrant any extra discount.

Financial disaster was however just around the corner for the new firm, which traded as Central Building Supplies. A bad business deal led to 400 overpriced 'perspex' acrylic baths having to be sold at a loss - which in turn led to the loss of Maurice Mosley's home when the bank refused to extend his credit. In the words of the bank manager 'You are most unlikely ever to make a profit, and I want repayment of the bank's loan to yourself'.

Others might have been daunted by the dreadful turn of events, but the conclusion drawn by Maurice was that there was money to be made from manufacturing acrylic baths. Tightening his belt a few extra notches and getting stuck in, working long hours Maurice took all kinds of jobs before setting up a small scale manufacturing plant, Trojan Plastics, on the upper floors of John Lockwood's Britannia Mills in Milnsbridge.

A load of second hand manufacturing equipment was acquired: vacuum pumps and a compressor, moulding rigs, special ovens for preheating the acrylic sheets, circular saws, glass-fibre spray equipment, routers, jigs and packaging.

Weariness and frustration were beginning to take hold. Understandably JMV Mosley was beginning to feel that whatever he did sooner or later he would be 'kicked in the teeth' and be back to square one again. But, like Scotland's Robert the Bruce inspired by the famous spider which wouldn't give up, Maurice was determined to try and try again.

The solution to the problem was easy: just cut out ICI and have Trojan manufacture its own acrylic sheet rather than buy it in.

But easier said than done! 'Total madness' in the company founder's own words. ICI had invested millions and employed highly skilled chemists to become the UK's only manufacture of acrylic sheet, which it did in a magnificent high tech plant.

Before those grandiose plans could be fully implemented however, another disaster struck Trojan.

A dishonest employee seeking to disguise his attempted theft of a bath now set fire to the five-storey mill; the result was one of the most spectacular blazes ever seen in the Colne Valley.

As if that shock were not enough Maurice Mosley, with large business debts hanging over him, having just bought Ashbrow Mills for acrylic sheet manufacture with a business loan, was the immediate suspect. How much did he benefit from the insurance the police demanded to know. Only when he explained that he had not been able to afford the absurd annual insurance premium of £100,000 for £100,000 of cover did the police console him with a cup of tea.

The arsonist was caught and jailed. Though much good that did Trojan Plastics. Many businesses would have simply folded at this point. Yet the business, by now a limited company, just managed to hold on at Ashbrow Mills (formerly the Crowther & Nicholson textile mill).

At Ashbrow Mills an entire acrylic sheet manufacturing business, trading as Lexcast, was being constructed from scratch. A steam-raising boiler, huge water baths 25 feet deep, and a massive crane were installed alongside polymerisation equipment and a chemical laboratory. The first attempt to produce acrylic sheet was catastrophic. In half an hour faulty control equipment had caused £50,000 worth of damage.

Happily on the second attempt some considerable time later, despite all the previous set backs, all went well. JMV Mosley's extraordinary tenacity and entrepreneur-ship would at last begin to pay off.

Top: A painting of Ramsden Mill painted in 1991 prior to the demolition of the old five storey mill.
***Above**: Seated from left to right: Ernie Hatton (Managing Director), J M V Mosley (Chairman and founder) and Robert Mosley (Trojan Production Manager). Standing from left to right: Mike Meitiner (Lexcast Chemist), Adam Mosley (Lexcast Chemist Manager), Barry Gerry (Trojan Production Manager), David Mosley (Sales and Marketing Manager) and Malcolm Senior (Lexcast Director).*

In 1979 Hartford Holdings Ltd was created to hold the vested interests of both Trojan and Lexcast. Other subsidiaries would follow.

Trojan continued to trade from Ashbrow mills for some years before moving to its current location in Ramsden Mills when its then occupants Taylor & Livesey Ltd decided to discontinue manufacturing and closed down.

In the following years production of acrylic sheeting, and from it baths and shower trays, would grow and grow, with at one time half of the business output going to export.

Aquacast Ltd, a manufacturer of stone resin shower trays, originally based in Halifax, was acquired in 1998. In the same year it was relocated to Milnsbridge in a temporary building. In 2001 it was moved into a newly built, state-of-the-art factory and has since seen continued growth as the demand for its products grows.

However by the end of the century, as a result of the strength of the pound, exports had fallen dramatically. The answer would be investment in another factory overseas.

A South African company based in Ladysmith - Plexicor (Pty) Ltd - which made baths and shower bases, was being put into receivership. In 2001 Trojan bought the business and found jobs for all the workers who had been laid off. More recently the whole business was moved to new 220,000 sq ft premises 120 miles away in Pietermaritzburg: all but four of the staff (including the tea lady) moved with the business. New equipment was installed; in three years business there trebled, double shifts are being worked. Some 70 per cent of output is exported to the Far East, Middle East the USA and the majority of countries in Europe; meanwhile back in Yorkshire Trojan has become one of the largest volume manufacture of acrylic baths in the United Kingdom. Trojan can potentially manufacture 10,000 baths and 9,000 bath panels a week combined with Plexicor the group could potentially manufacture 730,000 baths a year.

In time Trojan Plastics has become a member of a group of companies including not only Plexicor in South Africa, but also circular slide rule makers M H Mear & Co Ltd (based in Dalton, Huddersfield), Lexcast and Aquacast in Huddersfield, all within the Hartford Holdings Ltd group of companies.

Today the once tiny acorn is an industrial oak. Hartford Holdings owns a 36 acre site in Milnsbridge (Ramsden Mill) which houses two high volume bath plants, a newly developed shower tray plant (Aquacast Ltd) and recently M H Mear & Co Ltd., an 11 acre site in Fartown (Ashbrow Mills) which is home to Lexcast and a 10 acre site in Pietermaritzburg where Plexicor operates from. The group employs some 350 staff, in addition to the founder's sons Bob, David and Adam who are also involved within the group. Bob manages one of the bath plants at Milnsbridge, David works alongside Ernie Hatton (the current Managing Director) in Sales and Marketing and Adam is working at the Chemical processing plant.

And what better name for the company? There's no doubt that founder JMV Mosley had to work like the proverbial Trojan to finally triumph over all the many obstacles on his way to success.

Below: An aerial view of the Trojan Plastics site, 2005.

Syngenta - A vital role in feeding the world

The world's population increases by approximately 8,500 people each hour of each day. Every second - in the time it takes for you to click your fingers - there is another two extra people to feed and clothe.

The 6.5 billion people or so now inhabiting our planet rely on plants for food, clothing, fuel, shelter and medicine and it is vital to ensure that the world's crops reach their true potential to meet the needs of this expanding world population. However, even today with modern crop protection solutions, nearly one third of the world's crop production is still lost each year as a result of pests and diseases as less and less land has to provide more and more food. Without crop protection the losses would be massively higher and many more people would go without food and clothing.

For many years, products produced at the Syngenta Manufacturing Centre in Huddersfield have been at the forefront of this battle to protect the world's crops from the ravages of pests, weeds and diseases - helping growers across the globe to produce food, fibre and animal feedstuffs in a sustainable way.

The development of modern methods of crop protection has played a vital role during the last century in ensuring the continued improvement required to feed a world population that has grown from approximately 1.5 billion in 1900 to over four times this amount in the last 100 years. Economic growth during the same period has led to a greater demand for food of higher quality by consumers. In addition, the availability of a plentiful supply of fruit and vegetables, made possible by crop protection solutions and seeds varieties, has made a huge impact on human health in many countries over the past few decades. Modern pest control and other products are also helping to protect many millions of people across the world from health-threatening pests such as mosquitoes, cockroaches and rodents.

Top: Entrepreneur Read Holliday.
Below: An aerial view of the site in 1946.

Sustainable Agriculture provides a balanced approach to meet present and future needs and seeks to tailor the best available technologies to provide solutions to farming problems. This is where Syngenta's commitment lies, continuously improving farming through Sustainable Agriculture. As part of sustainable systems, crop protection products - fungicides, herbicides and insecticides - are an essential part of modern agriculture. They contribute to dramatic increases in yields and bring other benefits to people and the environment, by helping to produce the food and cloth that is needed to sustain a world population of over six billion.

The Syngenta team at the company's Leeds Road site in Huddersfield have contributed for many years to world agriculture, playing an important role in the provision of products to support these Sustainable Agriculture systems. By providing crop control products, the site has helped farmers achieve increased quantity and better quality yields in a sustainable way. However, the provision of these and other useful products is not a recent addition to Huddersfield, the history of the Syngenta site dates back to the First World War and spans several different company names.

Located in the foothills of the Pennines, Huddersfield is the largest town in England and boasts a history of manufacturing excellence. During Victorian times Huddersfield was one of the most prolific producers of worsted cloth in the world. It was that excellence which prompted Read Holliday, a Bradford-born entrepreneur, to develop a range of dyestuff products to support the textile industry. In 1916 after a period of industrial growth which saw many changes, the Huddersfield site was developed, occupying a 250 acre site which was once the original home of the Great Yorkshire Show.

Manufacturing began when, at the age of 21, entrepreneur Read Holliday set up in business to distil ammonia for use in the scouring of wool. To capitalise on the geography of his enterprise, he moved premises to sit alongside Huddersfield Gas Light Company on the east of the town centre at Turnbridge. Holliday seized the opportunity to use waste by-product, coal tar from the Gas works and produce Naptha to generate a range of innovative products such as the Naptha lamp.

Although not a chemist himself his ingenuity combined with his relationship with eminent chemists of the day enabled him to extend his range of coal tar by-products to the manufacture of early synthetic dyestuffs as well as ammonia, creosote, benzene and paint solvents.

Though by the end of the 19th century, Britain had a thriving chemicals industry, the world leader at that time was Germany. German chemists had been at the forefront of many important scientific discoveries and industrialists had been quick to commercially exploit those developments to manufacture pharmaceuticals, synthetics and dyestuffs. Exports were vast and many other countries were heavily dependant upon imports of chemicals from Germany.

Top: *A view inside the plant in the 1940s.*

ship of these companies, the Huddersfield site has grown in importance to become a key manufacturing centre for a wide range of chemical products, manufacturing for a global market.

The Huddersfield site has an impressive record of firsts to its credit. It was the first UK centre for making the man-made products Nylon and Terylene and is associated with a number of innovative medical and agricultural products including the herbicide 'Reglone'. Huddersfield was also the first manufacturing site to utilise computer control on its then state-of-the-art South Azo dye plant. The Site is accredited with the Queens Technology Award, Investors in People and more recently, the Chemical Industries Association Manufacturing Excellence Award.

As a consequence of the outbreak of the First World War in 1914 there was an immediate shortage of key chemicals in Britain, not least those used to make dyes for military uniforms. The Government's strategy required a huge boost in British chemical production, covering all aspects of the industry and, in 1915, the Government of the day brought together leading chemical manufacturers, of which Holliday dyes was one, to create a national dye industry, British Dyes Ltd.

One of the sites acquired was the 250 acre site at Leeds Road, adjacent to Holliday's Turnbridge Works and the manufacture of dyes began on what is now Syngenta's Huddersfield site.

Today however, gone are the manufacture of dyes, colours and chemicals for textiles; in their place is one of the most technologically advanced production facilities in the UK, focused primarily on the manufacture of intermediaries for many leading crop protection products.

With a global marketing reach Syngenta has become a major player in the fields of non-selective herbicides and insect control, and the business is investing in plant biotechnology to offer farmers alternative ways to protect and improve the yield and quality of their crops. As a leader in crop protection and as one of the top three producers of high-value commercial seeds, Syngenta plays a key role in feeding and protecting the world.

In 1919 British Dyes merged with Levinstein Ltd of Blackley in Manchester to form the British Dyestuffs Corporation Ltd, one of the four founder companies of ICI (Imperial Chemical Industries) at its inception in 1926.

The site has since operated under the ownership of pioneering and leading edge companies such as ICI, AstraZeneca and currently Syngenta. Under the steward-

Above: *A filter press for filtration of final dyestuff.*
Right: *Drums from 1940 labelled with their destination - places as far and wide as Buenos Aires to Bombay.*

The world demand for effective agricultural products is growing and the skills and experience of the Huddersfield workforce is helping to meet this demand. Among several key products, Huddersfield supplies two Syngenta blockbuster products to a global market, herbicide 'Gramoxone' and 'Karate' a market leader in insect control. Herbicides such as 'Gramoxone' control weeds which may threaten crop yields or compromise their quality and 'Karate' controls pests which damage crops and transmit disease.

Syngenta's success on a global platform is acknowledged locally too. As well as worldwide initiatives such as the Syngenta Foundation for Sustainable Agriculture, in the local community Syngenta helps deliver science and educational projects. Music and the arts are also part of Huddersfield's heritage and

Syngenta has a history of supporting several local activities such as North Stars Steele Orchestra, the Huddersfield Choral Society and Lawrence Batley Theatre.

Syngenta is exploiting innovative research and technology to provide sustainable agricultural solutions. These solutions allow growers across the world to realise the true potential of crops and to deliver high quality food for an ever-growing and ever more demanding world population. The site at Huddersfield continues to make a valuable contribution to help protect the world's food and fibre crops.

Top: *Laying of the foundation stone for new office block, 1951.*
Left: *Crowds flock into the plant for Open Day, 1985.*

JB Schofield & Sons - Any old iron

Back in the 1800s, long before recycling was heard of, the Schofield family were hard at work earning a living recycling: woollen waste, leather belting, wooden bobbins, anything that the textile industry could reuse. Today JB Schofield & Sons Ltd is still at it.

James Schofield was born in 1828. In 1876 he and his wife Elizabeth bought land and property at Greenhead, Linthwaite. The deeds for the land describe him as a woollen waste dealer, James died in 1892 with the property passing to his wife. Upon her death in 1908 Joe Benjamin (JB) Schofield one of James' four children paid £700 for the property and three acres of land and the business of JB Schofield was born, by now dealing in scrap metal.

The business is therefore even older than the 'established 1912' which appeared on the firm's vehicles.

Joe Schofield had four sons, two of whom, Norman and Stanley, took the opportunity in 1920 to buy another eight acres of land for £410. In 1941 Norman paid £800 to buy the rest of the family's share in the property at Greenhead.

The horse and cart had been the transport of the day, however in 1933, some 13 years after Joe's death, the first diesel-engined vehicle came along, YG8732, a Morris commercial. By 1954, following the lean post-war years, Norman, encouraged by sons Carl and George scraped the money together to buy the company's first new vehicle, a Perkins P6-engined Dodge 5-tonner.

Norman told his sons 'This is the last new wagon I'll ever buy'. He did however buy the business of W Oldcorn from his

Top: Greenhead in the early 1900s. Left: Norman Schofield and grandson Mark, 1960.

Sheffield's steelworks. Further afield, Skinningrove's famous steelworks in the northeast was a regular destination by both day and night. The 216 mile round trip was a long day's work for stalwart driver Harold Brown, a character and long time employee, who was familiar with most of the pub landlords en route from Greenhead to Skinningrove!

Another regular customer was the Dick Lane foundry of English Electric in Bradford, where Carl struck up a friendship with Harry Wilkinson, the purchasing manager. English Electric was to become the bedrock of Schofield's ferrous scrap metal business during the 1970s and 80s.

The cupolas at Dick Lane needed up to 800 tonnes a month of low phosphorous cast iron, this 'grade 17' cast iron was to be Schofield's speciality.

Carl persuaded Harry Wilkinson to accept grade 17 cast iron 'skull' broken small and blended with the other broken castings, brake drums and engines. Skull could be bought cheaper therefore raising the profit margin on the whole load. On top of this the breaking process was refined, a purpose-made breaking pit with

friend William 'Bill' Oldcorn . Involved in coal and general haulage W Oldcorn still trades from the same office as JB Schofield.

In 1964 Norman's death at the age of 67 led to Carl and younger brother George taking over the business with some stock but very little money. The brothers set about expanding the company forming JB Schofield & Sons Ltd. Larger vehicles, Foden, the best premium vehicle of that era was the chosen marque, and are still the vehicles of choice. A new crane with an electro magnet for handling the ferrous scrap metal, crawler excavators, wheeled loaders and crawler cranes were all acquired, with demolition and plant hire now being undertaken.

During the 1960s in the Colne Valley rows of stone weavers' cottages were being condemned and demolished, keeping the demolition equipment busy. Industrial demolition sites were also providing scrap metal for the scrap processing side of the business. Many new houses were being built from the stone and wood reclaimed from the destruction of the houses being replaced.

Back in the scrapyard at Greenhead, redundant machinery from the textile industry was being processed into feedstock for local foundries and

Top: W Oldcorn Ltd bought by Norman Schofield and still owned by the company today. *Above left:* From left to right: George Richard, Carl and Andrew Schofield snow clearing in 1979. *Below:* Two Schofield ploughs snow clearing on Chain Road, Marsden in February 1979.

thick steel bedded in tarmac meant that even in the depths of winter Schofield's cast iron was clean. Most other merchants were breaking in filthy conditions; a larger 1.25 tonne steel breaking ball, a crane with a 40ft jib meant that they could break material that others couldn't touch.

All incoming materials were analysed, checking for correct carbon, silicon and phosphorous levels; in fact up to 16 elements were checked. This extra information meant that Schofield's could more accurately blend the cast iron mix. By now there were separating and screening plants too, fed by Schofield's dragline and loading shovels separating the metal runnings from foundry sand, and a waste skip service taking waste to landfill sites. This was all to end in 1990 with the sudden closure for environmental reasons of the foundry.

The next generation of Schofields had started their working lives in the business during the 1970s, the first being Carl's eldest son Mark - George's sons Andrew, Richard and Michael all following later.

Now came local authority work. Carl had had a chance meeting with the area engineer for the newly formed West Yorkshire Metropolitan Council, Keith Dwyer, another of life's great characters. Carl was invited to tender for hire work including winter road maintenance - gritting , or better still snow ploughing. It became Carl's passion, almost a paid hobby, and a change from breaking cast iron.

By 1980 almost every piece of equipment Schofield's owned had been adapted to move snow: 16 bulk gritters, tippers with ploughs, crawler shovels, JCBs, everything and everybody was utilised, working to keep the trans-Pennine passes open.

Many of the gritters that Schofield's used were unique, built and modified in their own workshops, sandblasted and sprayed by Mark with the most effective rust preventative paint; the vehicles were never less than smart even though new vehicles couldn't be justified on council rates of pay. Most of the time it made a profit and most of the time, most of the workforce enjoyed doing it. There were occasions however when with his diesel frozen and waxy, salt frozen solid (yes it does freeze) hands and feet colder still, a driver might long to be home in bed. For Carl one of the problems with gritting was that his stocks of cast iron, pre-broken ready for delivery, would dwindle whilst he was out in his snowplough. To counter that risk, year on year the piles grew bigger and the roadways around the site narrower; by the time Dick Lane foundry closed there was enough stock for around two years melting left.

Schofield's remote rural hill top location means that scrap has to be sourced from far and wide therefore modern reliable transport has to be the order of the day. Schofield's smartly kept high-spec Fodens have been a familiar sight on the northern roads for over 40 years; these vehicles along with the gritters have been featured in several heritage commercial magazine articles with words and photographs supplied from keen amateur photographer Mark's archive of over 50,000 photographs.

Top: *A Sennebogen scrap handler machine, Schofield's were the first in the country to have this machine.* **Left:** *Carl Schofield pictured with the new Foden in 1985.*

The Greenhead site has seen much modernisation over the years, a non-ferrous sorting shop, a four-bay vehicle workshop, tarmac roadways, new weighbridge, site concrete, drainage, the introduction of strict health and safety rules and environmental legislation, and IT systems; each in its turn affecting the working lives of the Schofield family. Mark's two sons, another Carl and John (another JB), are now establishing themselves in the family business of recycling.

Schofield's legendary mountains of scrap seem never to change, in reality though much of the incoming material is processed and loaded for export the same day, only the higher grade foundry material being stockpiled until orders are received.

The markets for recycled scrap metal have changed dramatically during the last 10 years, traditionally scrap sales would be split 80-90% for home consumption with the rest going to export, now the opposite is true. Schofield's does however still supply most of the area's foundries, the large stocks ensuring that material is available no matter how large the order.

As for the future, it's more of the same. Changes in legislation are challenges that have to be met - just like the weather. The site is a pleasant place to work in summer but

a challenging environment in winter - the rain usually being horizontal and travelling at 60mph.

But challenging or not Greenhead has been home as well as work to six generations of the Schofield family, any plans to expand into nearby towns have invariably been scuppered because none of them want to work anywhere else.

Top: *A birds eye view of Greenhead in 1987.*
Below: *Part of the Schofield fleet of Fodens.*

Armitage Sykes LLP - The lawyers' tale

The modern solicitor is the successor to three former ancient professions known as attorneys, solicitors and proctors. In earlier times these 'lawyers' assisted judges on the Kings Bench in the early stages of litigation, or carried out the less-skilled work in the ecclesiastical and Admiralty courts.

Successive reorgan-isations of the courts of law and of the legal profes-sion have left us with just two kinds of lawyers: barristers and solicitors.

For most people barristers remain remote ethereal people whose work is seldom understood by those outside the law. By contrast solicitors are familiar folk with offices on every high street.

Sooner or later we all become involved in matters legal: making a will, buying a house or getting divorced.

For those in business solicitors offer even more help: partnership agreements, company formation, debt collection, employment disputes and, sometimes, bankruptcy.

In Huddersfield one of the most familiar names is the firm of Armitage Sykes LLP, a firm of solicitors whose history in the town goes back far beyond the memory of anyone now living.

Indeed, almost as if to underline the point, the very names Armitage and Sykes are historically speaking two of the most common family names in the area.

Above and right: *Former members of Hall Norton & Atkins.*

As long ago as 1750 the forerunner of Armitage Sykes LLP solicitors was practising law in Huddersfield; back then however the name of the firm was Crosland & Fenton.

Today Crosland & Fenton's papers are held by the West Yorkshire Kirklees archive service. Those papers include draft wills dating back to 1808; there are also court briefs for clients, including businesses and townships, dating from 1763 to 1840; there are deeds, rental and other papers relating to the Storthes Hall Estate from 1846 to1926; Penistone manor court baron rolls from 1811 to 1935; various clients' deeds, draft deeds and abstracts of title from as far back in time as 1718 - and including proper-ties as far apart as Brighouse, Greetland, Heckmondwike, Mirfield, Rastrick, Saddleworth, Shelley, Shepley, Thurstonland, and of course every part of Huddersfield.

Not for them the modern day rush of completing complicated commercial transactions or handling tricky matrimonial disputes. More likely there would have been a leisurely and scholarly approach to the complex and arcane application of the law at that time. Justice and law have sadly not always been synonymous, still more so in those far off days. Mr Crosland practised from Deadmanstone near Berry Brow, Huddersfield, later moving to King Street. From that legal practice arose in due course the firm of Hall, Norton & Atkins who practised from 9 Station Street, Huddersfield until their amalgamation in 1993 with the younger, but still venerable, firm of Armitage, Sykes & Hinchcliffe.

Armitage, Sykes and Hinchcliffe, according to conversations recorded with Mr Paul Bradley and Mr Herbert E Walker, respectively Clerk and Articled Clerk (trainee solicitor) to Mr Walter Armitage, began life around 1850.

In the mid-19th century Mr Armitage lived as a country gentleman at Kirkstyles Farm, Cumberworth, a farm of about 70 acres in the southern rural outskirts of the town. He kept a fine table and a good cellar, but any money made in the law was lost on the farm. He made the journey from Cumberworth to Huddersfield astride a white horse which he stabled at a hostelry in Lord Street. It is said that Mr Armitage would fight a case all day for a guinea. Mr James Sykes joined him in 1891 and Mr AET Hinchcliffe soon after then.

Until around this time the formal education of solicitors often left much to be desired.

In 1899 however, after earlier unsuccessful initiatives in 1879-80 and in 1888-89, law teaching was eventually introduced into the curriculum of the Yorkshire College (Leed's University's predecessor).

Above: Armitage Sykes & Hinchcliffe circa 1910.

Mr Armitage had died in 1898 (the day after he made his will - not a good example to his clients) and the office moved to 13 Westgate, now a building society office, before moving to 1 Westgate over Lloyds Bank, where the firm would stay for some 60 years until 1973. It is said that there was considerable rivalry for the tenancy of 1 Westgate, which was then owned by the West Yorkshire Bank before its takeover by Lloyds. However, the fact that Mr James Sykes' uncle Sir Charles Sykes of Brockholes was a director of the bank may have made a difference.

Before the Great War of 1914-18 the personnel was of course all male - including the secretaries or clerks. But the war changed all that and the first female secretaries started work in around 1920. The firm is perhaps more distinguished for providing one of the first (of four) women to qualify as solicitors in 1925 - namely Mary Sykes. Women were in fact only permitted to become solicitors in 1922. Mary Sykes was the daughter of James Sykes and later went on to found her own practice. The story goes that she was eventually constrained to resign from the firm when AET Hinchcliffe persisted in correcting the duplicates of the letters she had sent the previous day - that was the final straw. In those days the senior partner still saw all the duplicates of letters sent from the office, no matter who had written them.

The Yorkshire Board of Legal Studies (representing local Law Societies) offered the College an annual grant of £450 if it would undertake to establish a Law Department in order to prepare candidates for University degrees and professional examinations.

Some 22 students were enrolled. Initially, most of the students were part-time non-degree students, who studied for one year in preparation for the Law Society's Intermediate Examination while working as articled clerks in solicitors' offices. There were only a handful of law degree students. They too also worked as articled clerks, while studying for three years for the degree which gave exemption from the Law Society's Intermediate Examination.

The Department's first graduate was James Sykes of Huddersfield, who passed the Final LL.B. examinations in June 1902.

One of the consequences of the firm's great longevity is the inheritance of the management of ancient charitable trusts like the Godfrey Beaumont Charity, originally set up to provide a stipend for the parishes of Meltham and Honley. There was also the Robert Nettleton Charity founded in 1613. All that experience has been of considerable assistance in welding the present generation of

*Top: Walter Armitage, former partner of Armitage Sykes & Hinchcliffe. **Above right:** Mr A E T Hinchcliffe.*

lawyers into a cohesive team, with competence over a wide area of practice rarely found in a comparatively small provincial town. The firm was even involved in 1853 in efforts to unseat the sitting Member of Parliament. History fails to relate the outcome of this, but it must have progressed quite far as there is a letter reporting the arrangements made for the various witnesses to travel to London for a hearing.

Lawyers most readily learn their trade by sitting at the feet of others in the firm who can show them how things are done. Old established firms can do this. But we must not look solely at the past. Modern technology, particularly the fulsome use of electronic messaging and the rapid exchange of information have transformed the way modern solicitors do business. Armitage Sykes LLP was the first legal firm in Huddersfield to embrace the computer, something which makes possible a far greater efficiency in dealing with the modern client's requirements in business and private matters. From its ancient roots the practice has grown into a decidedly modern firm, now practising from 72 New North Road, 4 Macaulay Street and at Brighouse and Elland. But despite its modernity the firm's histor-

ical reputation is something which all in the practice are proud to preserve.

That reputation counts for a great deal: over 90 per cent of the firm's business comes from existing clients or word of mouth recommendations.

Today Armitage Sykes LLP has expertise in over 44 specialist legal areas through its seven departments staffed by 25 lawyers. The experience of these specialists enables them to understand everyone's concerns and anxieties and to maximise clients' chances of a successful outcome.

For over 250 years Armitage Sykes LLP has played a significant role in the communal and business life of Huddersfield. Now in the 21st century the firm is one of the largest in the area, providing decisive legal advice, guidance and solutions to over 10,000 individual, business and organisational clients all of whom who value the high standard of legal support they receive.

Below: *The firms current premises.*

Wood Auto's - Sparks to parts

Wood Auto Supplies Ltd, a Huddersfield company that has been involved with auto-electrics for some 80 years, was founded in the 1920s by Reginald Wood who traded originally as 'Wood the Battery Man'. The first Certificate of Incorporation is dated 1929.

The year 1929 was perhaps the least auspicious year in the whole of the twentieth century in which to start a business. The year saw the Wall Street crash, the starting gun for the great depression which would see millions thrown on the dole as factory after factory closed.

But the misery was not evenly spread; some industries were decimated, others just managed to tick along. And yet others, the most buoyant and growing part of industry, actually managed to weather the storm in relative comfort.

One area of endeavour which was less affected than most was the automotive industry, an industry still in its infancy and one which was still growing despite the economic recession.

As a result of the resilience of the motoring sector Reginald Wood had made a good choice when starting his own business.

Reginald Wood was set to become an influential force in the town; he would even become Mayor of Huddersfield in the 1950s. The youngest of a family of 14 children, Reginald's earlier career as an ammunitions inspector had first brought him to Huddersfield from his home town of Huntingdon.

Oliver Cromwell hailed from Huntingdon, and, although the company moved its location over the years it has always retained the name 'Cromwell Works'.

In the very early years Reginald was assisted by his three daughters, Vera, Molly and Peggy. The company began to specialise in rewinding automotive components, and those skills were put to good use during the war years.

After the war Reginald's two sons, John and Walter came back to Huddersfield and began developing the merchandising side of the business.

Having outgrown its premises, the original firm and the winding operation was moved from Standard House to Portland Street, opposite the old Royal Infirmary. This business became Wood Auto Supplies Ltd which concentrated on the manufacture of armatures, field coils, dynamos and starter motors. The company expanded under the direction of John Wood and Douglas Heywood who had been one of Reginald's first apprentices when he left school in 1930.

In the meantime John's younger brother, Walter, developed the Factoring Division which continues to supply local garages and fleet users with spare parts, accessories, paints and test equipment.

Top: Reginald Wood. *Right:* A Wood's display stand at the 1952 Earl's Court Motor Show.

the throne; later that same year the New Elizabethan Age became the Atomic Age when Britain exploded its first nuclear bomb. The mood of the country changed from one of seemingly relentless pessimism to one of new optimism.

And out of that optimism came renewed business confidence. In the following years the British standard of living would rise year on year - and in the wake of that increase came ever-increasing use of motor vehicles. Inevitably the prospects of the ably managed Wood Autos rose with that tide of national prosperity.

The Wood Auto Supplies factory moved to Fitzwilliam Street in 1960, and again in 1980 to Colne Road, opposite Wood Auto Factors branch. Today Wood Auto Supplies exports to more than 70 countries from Huddersfield.

In recent years the business has formed alliances with overseas manufacturers whose products supplement the traditional homemade range to fit passenger cars, commercial and agricultural vehicles, marine and off road applications of almost every make and origin.

Wood Auto is still a private independent company with a proud history and confident of its future as a major force in the world of auto-electrics.

Top left: An early view of the factory showing the efficiency and skill of the workers, an important factor in the continuing success of the company. ***Above left:*** Wood's fully stocked warehouse. ***Below:*** Woods' Cromwell Works.

The immediate post-war years were ones of austerity. Petrol was still rationed and new vehicles hard to come by with long waiting lists for delivery.

Nationally the economy was in the doldrums, and worse a huge debt had been incurred to the USA as a way of financing the second world war. The Government saw exports as the way out of the problem and made strenuous attempts to encourage all firms to export more.
In 1952 in a successful attempt to raise its profile the company took a stand at the Motor Show. And export opportunities followed; the first orders coming from Australia and Turkey.

Curiously 1952 would be the year that Britain at last turned the corner. A new monarch Queen Elizabeth II ascended to

Merrie England - Roast beef and coffee

The Merrie England of the historical past was famous for its roast beef. But these days the name is associated even more with coffee. Today's Merrie England, based in Huddersfield's Kirkgate, was founded more than 30 years ago. Then the first Merrie England premises had just half a dozen staff; now in the 21st century, what has grown to become Merrie England Coffee Shops Ltd, employs more than 150 full and part time staff.

Of course coffee shops have been around for a very long time. The first coffee shops began to appear in London as long ago as the 17th century, many being used as places of business by their customers: the London Stock Exchange for example traces its origins to trading which took place between customers who once frequented the same coffee shop.

The American revolutionaries famously objected to paying tax on tea, an objection dramatically illustrated at the 'Boston tea party' in which the cargo of tea clippers was tipped into Boston harbour. Less action-minded Americans who objected to the

tea tax voted with their teacups and simply switched to drinking coffee instead.

In the 19th century tea became indisputably the national drink of Britain and coffee was relegated to a minor role in life. In the 1950s however, a new fascination with all things American, not least rock and roll music, saw a resurgence of interest in that quintessential American drink coffee, and with that interest came the coffee bar. From having once been home to financial speculators coffee bars now became the haunt of would-be pop stars such as Cliff Richard

Above: *January 1970, the first three cups of coffee served at the Merrie England, 18 Kirkgate. Founders Nita and Keith Hanselman with Mr Kenneth Barlow, the Catering Advisor of the Yorkshire Electricity Board. The first Italian Gaggia Coffee machine in Yorkshire imported from Italy by The Merrie England Coffee Shops Ltd can just be seen in between the founders.* **Below:** *The first Merrie England, opened in January 1970. The premises were however demolished in 1971 to make way for the Pack Horse development.*

stopped work: customers were still served by staff operating by candle light and cooking on camping gas - curiously customers actually seemed to like it and came in even larger numbers.

Later Merrie England would mark another first in Yorkshire. Long before MacDonald's arrived on the scene Merrie England had introduced the drive in window from the USA. Previously customers had got out of their cars and knocked on the window to be served, sometimes in the pouring rain. It took months before drivers learnt to drive up for their takeaway orders: today however they have got the hang of it and there are queues of cars waiting for their take out orders.

and Tommy Steel who would famously gave their inaugural performances in London's Two I's coffee bar.

But Brylcreme and jukeboxes alone would not be enough to sustain coffee bar culture. Many opened in the 1950s and 1960s only to later close.

How then did Merrie England, an institution which has now become part of our traditional town centre scene, thrive?

Company founders were Keith and Nita Hanselman. In the late 1960s they were running D'Agostino's ice cream makers and snack bar in the Market Hall and Beast Market.

In 1970 the couple opened the first Merrie England at 14 Kirkgate, the former premises of Oldfield & Studdards. It was a short lived occupancy - just 12 moths later the premises would be demolished to make way for the new Packhorse development.

The first year was however a fine learning experience. And a reputation for excellence and innovation was earned when the pair imported a Gaggia coffee machine from Italy, the first in Yorkshire, whilst simultaneously offering Merrie England's famous beef sandwiches at half a crown (12 $^{1/2}$ p) a time.

In subsequent years shoppers, town centre workers and retired folk would make a bee line to Merrie England knowing they would get the best. Freshly made coffee, made from beans ground to order, was a specialty. And each night topside of beef was, and still is, slow roasted to ensure that only the finest ingredients find their way into Merrie England's sandwiches alongside their famous homemade apple pies.

Providing only the best quality in clean and friendly surround-ings and a 'Merrie England smile' was to prove a winning formula. Not even the power cuts during the Miners' strike

Merrie England Coffee Shops are now run by Keith and Nita's daughters Lisa and Gina, they are working hard to ensure that the Merrie England tradition of excellence is being experienced by an ever increasing numbers of satisfied customers.

Above: *The second branch of the Merrie England which opened four months after the shop at 18 Kirkgate, 1970. Situated between Freeman Hardy Willis and Woolworth's on Commercial Street in Brighouse was formally a gents outfitters.* **Below:** *The familiar sight of a busy Merrie England at the company's Halifax shop.*

W Fisher & Son - Off the wall

Tiles have been popular since Roman times. They are immensely strong and hardwearing. Visitors to Italy even today who go to inspect Roman ruins more than 2,000 years old can see that tiled floors and mosaics can survive almost undamaged for centuries.

Julius Caesar landed in Britain in 55 BC and for the next 400 years Roman tiles would become a feature of British homes as well, until the Dark Ages ushered in centuries when tile technology was lost.

Happily that technology was not lost forever: the industrial revolution of the 18th and 19th centuries saw a new upsurge in ceramics and in the mid 19th century a new golden age of tiling arrived, many marvellous examples of which can be seen in private and public buildings today.

The Huddersfield firm of W Fisher & Sons (Tilers) Ltd hasn't been going quite long enough to have been involved in helping the Romans tile their villas, but it still has a century and a half of history behind it.

The roots of the business can be traced back to 1860 when Leonard Fisher moved from the small village of

Top left: Founder Leonard Fisher.
Above: The W Fisher & Sons workforce pictured in 1937. Founder Walter Fisher is seated centre with sons Eric centre left and Leonard centre right, also pictured is Bert Ovenden Walter's son-in-law, back centre .

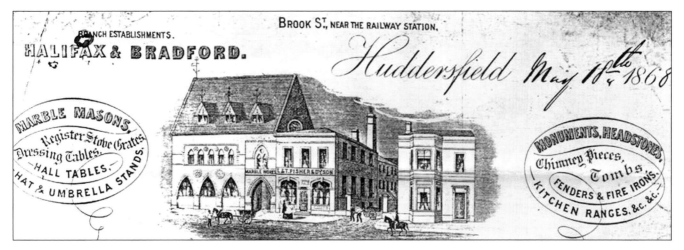

Sibthorpe in Nottinghamshire to Huddersfield. Leonard Fisher was a seventh son who in turn would have seven sons himself: the seventh being given the appropriate name of Septimus. Here in Huddersfield Leonard joined a monumental mason in Brook Street to further his career as a sculptor and monumental mason carving stone and marble.

Leonard worked closely with the head carver, an Italian of inebriate habits who one day disappeared back to Italy leaving behind a large unfinished statue. Leonard finished the work and in completing the fine detail on the statue to such a high standard that he was promoted to head carver.

When the owner retired Leonard took over the business and was joined by his brother Thomas Fisher as well as a partner named Dyson whose name features on early bill-heads. By 1868 the firm had grown considerably with branches in Halifax and Bradford. The Huddersfield premises in Brook Street still exist with the words MARBLE WORKS carved over the entrance.

Leonard's son Walter Fisher was trained by his father and continued the business through the first world war, working from smaller rented premises in Friendly Street, at the rear of the Friendly and Trades Society's building. In recent years those premises have been converted into living accommodation.

In his turn Walter had two sons, the eldest another Leonard, and the younger Eric.

During the second world war Eric, the apple of his father's eye, worked furiously tiling at Britain's many new airfields in Yorkshire and Lincolnshire before tragically dying of a brain haemorrhage whilst tiling the frontage of a theatre in Leicester.

Leonard became Huddersfield's first glider pilot. During the second world war he was a commissioned flying officer, training the glider pilots to fly the giant hawsers favoured by Winston Churchill to silently land troops and small armoured vehicles behind enemy lines in the invasion of Europe.

After the war Leonard Fisher expanded his ceramic wall and floor tiling activities into decorative floor coverings such as linoleum, rubber and thermoplastics

The company is well known in the town having tiled countless thousands of kitchens and bathrooms as well as much larger projects, such as the old hospital on Portland Street (now Huddersfield Technical College) and the Huddersfield Infirmary at Lindley, a major project involving 10,000 square metres of wall tiles.

Leonard's son Peter Eric Fisher had left Almondbury Grammar School at the age of 17 and worked on the Infirmary project whilst serving his apprenticeship.

With some regret and a touch of embarrassment Peter today admits to having a secret ambition in his early twenties to fly for a career, as an airline pilot. The ambition may well have been stimulated by his father's experience as a civilian glider pilot which had served the country so well during the war years when he became a flying officer in the RAF.

At the age of 24 Peter successfully applied for and was offered a commission in the RAF to fly heavy aircraft which he viewed as a stepping stone to his aspiration for a career as a civil airline pilot.

Regrettably this ambition was not to be fulfilled as family commitments would block his path. During Peter's nine years away from the family business

Top: An early letterhead dated 1868.

working for a similar company in Chester owned by an ex-para he was inspired to take up the sport, parachuting initially at Half Penny Green airport near Wolverhampton, with later free-fall training at Nether-avon in Wiltshire, the home of the Army Parachute Association.

On his return to the family business Peter continued to parachute and qualified as an instructor at what was then the Parachuting Club which operated from Leeds/Bradford Airport.

Having worked in London and Chester for several years, at the age of 30 Peter returned to Huddersfield in 1975.

Peter's return was well timed: soon afterwards his father Leonard suffered a stroke. For several years Peter worked a 14-hour day seven days a week to create a much needed revival in the firm's fortunes.

During the following 20 years, besides training thousands of parachuting students Peter carried out parachute display exhibitions at hundreds of venues throughout Huddersfield, Yorkshire and the United Kingdom beside competing at both national and international level representing the UK in many European countries. In 1979 his team won a gold medal at the British National Parachuting Championships, ironically held that year at Netheravon where he had carried out most of his basic training nine years earlier. That achieve-ment involved competing against not only civilian free-fall parachutists from the UK but also the RAF Falcons and the Red Devils, the latter being the most famous top British Army team.

Sadly Peter would be forced to give up his parachuting activities in 1995 after having suffered a slight stroke: in his preceding 25 years involvement in the sport he had completed 2,000 freefall parachute descents.

Following the death of Leonard Fisher in 1984 additional office space was rented in St Peter's Street adjacent to the company showroom in what was then the YMCA building in Northumberland Street, whilst still retaining the original warehouse premises in Friendly Street.

In 1988 however, the Northumberland Street showroom was set ablaze by an arsonist. The arsonist carried out no fewer than 16 such attacks throughout the town, causing considerable destruction before finally being apprehended by the long arm of the law and sentenced to three years imprisonment in Armley jail.

Though the arsonist may have been caught and jailed that was little comfort to Peter Fisher and his employees. The setback nearly finished the business. Peter however recalled his grandfather's sage advice 'when the going gets tough the tough get going'. Over the next two years, after an immense struggle, both financial and physical, Peter Fisher bought and completely renovated the firm's current premises at 100-102 Northgate, a

Top and Above: *Walter Fisher, Master Tiler who formed the Limited company (top) and Leonard Fisher also a Master Tiler (above).*

techniques, inventing and patenting sophisticated equipment, which revolutionised large-scale tile laying methods. In 1999 the Department of Trade and Industry bestowed upon the company a Merit Award for Research & Technology.

Alongside his lifetime's commitment to tiling Managing Director Peter Fisher is also a keen potter producing ceramic ware in the pottery studio in the basement at Northgate.

Road works along Bradford Road in 2005 resulted in large amounts of clay being excavated, some of which was subsequently used to make hundreds of pots fired in a kiln literally only a few feet away, many of which were subsequently sold at the Holmfirth Art Exhibition.

property previously occupied by Lunn & Cardno, Decorators, and before then by Fred Tetlow & Son, Sporting Equipment Suppliers. Even earlier the building had been the Huddersfield North Ward Liberal Club headquarters, and earlier still the Cobden Club started by Richard Cobden, Liberal MP famous for his successful anti-corn law campaign.

During the 1990s the company changed significantly, concentrating on offering the widest range of quality ceramics from around the world, and floor coverings to the local domestic market. Large-scale industrial work was also undertaken for all the major car manufacturers, the medical and pharmaceutical industry, and over 50 supermarkets for one client alone.

The company made enormous technological advances by adapting and mechanising industrial floor tiling

Top and Above: Peter Fisher, front, with staff in 1990 at the opening of the present premises, pictured below.

Drakes - Called to the bar

For those who like a pint, or even those who simply enjoy a soft drink in the company of friends, there is no finer institution than the English public house. Our hospitable hotels, inns and humble pubs are the envy of the world.

People have written whole books about them. Real ale guides abound. In 2005 one enterprising chap even completed a lifetime's ambition, not to say lifetime's work, of having a drink in every real ale pub in the CAMRA list. Others have written books on the complex social rules encountered in pubs: how to get served at a crowded bar, and how many times you have to visit a pub to be counted a regular. But no one yet seems to have written a book on pub furniture.

That's a pity. Pub furniture is curiously corporate yet at the same time homely and familiar.

How many times have you sat on a bar stool or been ensconced in wooden settle? How many times have you sank a pint in a sunny beer garden and put down your empty glass on a three-legged cast iron table?

So familiar are these items that we almost forget they are there; yet where did the pub get them from? You don't usually see them for sale in the high street.

A local business which could answer that question very easily for us is Drakes Bar Furniture.

Drakes Bar Furniture, based at Cliffe Commercial Park at Longroyd Bridge has been in business for more than a quarter of a century. Today Drakes' bespoke and standard bar furniture has acquired an international reputation.

Top: Founder John Drake.
Right: Partner Neil Bettson.

The company was founded in 1980 by John Drake and was then based at Farrar Mills, at Salterhebble in Halifax.

An apprentice-trained joiner, John was 20 years old when he took up the challenge of setting up his own business.

In those days the company turnover was £36,000, with John as the sole worker; after meeting expenses his wage was £85 per week for 60 hours!

At that time the nature of the business was general joinery; John's dream car was a Ford Cortina Ghia with a vinyl roof; unhappily however, the company could not run to such extravagances.

In 1996 John met up with 40-year-old Neil Bettson whose background was also as an apprentice trained joiner, though in his case one specialising in pub furniture. Neil took over the day-to-day running of the company when John's daughter Sophie was diagnosed with cancer at eighteen months old.

nationwide, but it also exports to more than seven other countries including the USA and Russia.

Not only do British pubs, inns and hotels provide a market for what is collectively termed 'bar furniture' but there is a growing international demand. As one might expect there are ex-pats throughout the world who long for a drink in a traditional English pub and seek to create such refuges in far flung corners of the globe. But demand doesn't all come from British exiles. Folk of all nationalities who have visited Britain and experienced the delights of the traditional British pub are equally keen to try and replicate its glories on their return home. In the 21st century the oh-so-familiar British pews and benches, bar stools and tables can be found in a surprising number of far away locations

Today Drakes Bar Furniture Ltd has an annual turnover of more than a million pounds: Neil Bettson drives a Bentley, whilst John Drake has forgotten all about that Ford Cortina with the vinyl roof and instead drives an Aston Martin!

Top: One of the company's selection of fixed seating. Above left: Drakes themed seating combination. Below: A company delivery van.

With Neil looking after the business the company changed direction and plunged into the pub industry market.

Neil's inclination to move the company in the direction in which he had served his apprenticeship would prove a wise business move. The economy was good, as a result more people were frequenting pubs and so providing owners with increased profits and the wherewithal to buy new furniture. Furthermore, changes in the law led to pubs changing hands more frequently than before, again stimulating demand for refurbishing.

Within a year the company was enjoying a turnover of £500,000 and had ten employees. The business moved to Huddersfield in 1998. The company now delivers

Taylor & Lodge -Clothing the world

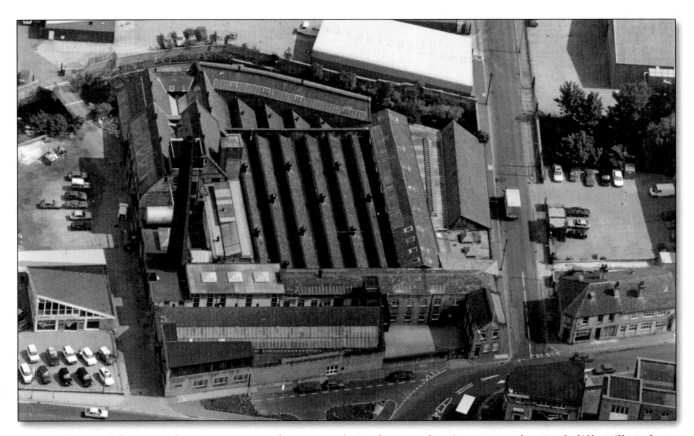

There can't be many obvious connections between Huddersfield and Norfolk. One which does spring to mind however is worsted cloth. The word comes from the Norfolk town of Worstead, which in the Middle-ages was famous for its fine smooth yarn made from combed long-staple wool. Today Huddersfield is famed for its production of the close-textured cloth which has long been known as worsted.

Weaving has been going on in the Huddersfield area for centuries. Records indicate that there was a Roger the Fuller (Fulling is a process where the woollen material was pounded in water to make it thicken) living at Holme in 1274.

In 1727 when Daniel Defoe visited the town he noted that woollen goods were being produced in abundance.

Since the 1960s many of Huddersfield's weaving mills have closed down, victims of recession and foreign competition. But as always there remains room at top, ensuring that the best have survived. One of the world's leading worsted manufacturers is Taylor & Lodge.

Taylor & Lodge, incorporated as Rashcliffe Mills Ltd, was founded in Huddersfield in 1883. It has occupied Rashcliffe Mills at Albert Street in Lockwood for more than a century. The company still carries out all aspects of fine worsted cloth production, using a combination of traditional methods and skills and, when it can be seen to enhance quality, it also applies the best of modern technology.

In the warp preparation room a fully automatic 'Uster' drawing machine is used, the first of its kind to be operated in the UK textile industry.

High speed 'Dornier' rapier looms in the weaving department ensure the precision and accuracy which is essential in the production of fine micron wool cloths, using superfine worsted yarn counts.

In 'finishing' however, traditional methods prevail. Taylor & Lodge still uses the very soft natural water from the

Top: Rashcliffe Mills, the home of Taylor & Lodge for over one hundred years.

River Holme, the moorland stream which flows alongside Rashcliffe Mills. All pieces are washed in conventional wooden machines using natural soap and pure local water, the same ingredients which for centuries have given Huddersfield its reputation as undisputed world leader in the production of fine worsted cloths. In the time-honoured way paper-pressing completes the finish by imparting the gentle lustre and delicate touch for which Taylor & Lodge cloths are renowned.

Fabric weights produced range from 165 grammes per square metre to 700 gms. Computerised pattern weaving looms make the sample production unit one of the most modern in the country. A large selection of suiting, jacketing and dishdasha cloths is created each season. No doubt at this point many readers will be

reaching for their dictionaries and asking themselves 'what is a dishdasha?', The word serves to underline the truly international scope of Taylor & Lodge's business - a dishdasha is the long robe with sleeves frequently worn by men on the Arabian peninsula and further afield.

A selection of cloths is shown at international exhibitions such as Premiere Vision in Paris, and during shows in London, Tokyo, Seoul, Hong Kong, Shanghai and New York.

More than 80 per cent of production is exported to around 20 countries, the main markets being Japan, the Far and Middle East and Europe. A very active design and marketing policy is pursued: all customers are visited regularly by the company's Managing Director and Design Director who are frequent overseas travellers.

Only natural fibres are used in production; the main ones being superfine wool, cashmere, silk and summer kid mohair, as well as rare fibres such as mink, sable, ermine and vicuna. The company is a founder member of the Lumb's Huddersfield Golden Bale Club and is still very proud to be a user of those hand-sorted wools. The company is also a member of the British Escorial Wool Guild and the Australian Superfine Wool Growers' Association.

In 1966 the company won the Queen's Award for Exporting, becoming the very first textile concern to receive it. Today Taylor & Lodge is deservedly recognised as the manufacturer of the finest and most luxurious cloths in the world.

In April 2005 the company was acquired by the Bradford based Bulmer and Lumb Group, so helping ensure not only the long term future of the local workforce of around 50, but also Huddersfield's reputation as the home of the world's finest worsted cloth.

This page: *View inside Taylor & Lodge's weaving department, Managing Director Gordon Kaye picture left, centre.*

A *Swift service*

What's the link between Huddersfield and Venice? The obvious answer would be that Venice is famous for its canals and so is Huddersfield. But though Huddersfield folk might be reluctant to claim that their canal is better than those in Venice the town can at least truthfully claim that it makes more and better Venetian blinds than the inhabitants of the Venice ever dreamed of.

The firm of Swift Blinds and Curtains was founded in 1969. Its home today is Aldon Works in Lockwood Road, the 11,000 sq ft premises which were acquired in 1988, with additional manufacturing space of 13,000 sq ft in Albert Street.

The company was founded by Alan Swift; he was born in Halifax in 1933 where his father had a bakery business.

Alan himself ran a bakery business in Wigan before selling it in 1963 to buy the Lepton Post Office and a grocery store, which he ran with is wife Pat.

During the mid 1960s, as a side line, Alan began selling and fitting carpets under the trading name of Aldon Carpets. The Aldon name still continues: when the blind business eventually became a limited company in 1976 it did so under the name Aldon Manufacturing (Hudd) Ltd trading as Swift Blinds.

From the outset the business was mainly selling and installing venetian blinds, which the firm subsquently

Top: Founder Alan Swift.
Below: Swift Blinds Cross Church Street showroom, 1979.

Originally there was a very limited range of patterns and designs, today the choice is vast.

Today the firm is retailing from a new extended showroom in Lockwood and from a showroom in Sheffield. As well as selling direct to the public the firm also supplies other curtain and blind retailers nation-wide. One speciality is venetian blinds for office partitioning. Another specialist product is solar control blinds used on ship's navigation bridges and supplied to shipping companies world wide.

Clients include the Huddersfield public, soft furnishings retailers, construction companies, schools and local authorities. Contract installation teams provide a service nation-wide.

made itself. It still makes more of these than any other kind of blind but now also produces vertical blinds, roller blinds, wood and soft cloth blinds for the home as well as blinds, canopies and awnings for shops, offices and other commercial and industrial applications.

In 1969 however the business, still included running the Post Office too and was run by just Alan and Pat Swift. Today the firm has more than 50 staff.

From the Lepton Post Office in Wakefield Road Alan and Pat opened a retail shop in Cross Church Street Huddersfield in 1979. The office and workroom moved from Lepton to Skelmanthorpe in 1980, and then to Silver Court Aspley in 1984 before eventually moving to the firm's current base in 1988.

Alan and Pat's son Nicolas joined the firm in 1976 when the business first began to manufacture venetian and roller blinds. Caroline Clegg, who later married Nicolas, also joined the firm in the same year. Alan and Pat's youngest son Christian joined the business in 1984 followed by his wife Heather.

Customers are guaranteed quality and satisfaction with the knowledge than in 1993 the company gained BS5750 Quality Assurance - becoming one of the first blind makers in the country to do so.

Today the business is run by Nicolas and Christian Swift as Joint Managing Directors.

Sadly Chairman and founder Alan Swift passed away two years after retiring in 1996 and Caroline after battling with M S most of her working life sadly died in 2003. The next generation of Swifts are all girls, Nicolas's daughter Alexia is currently at university whilst Christian's two daughters Georgina and Daniele are at school.

Shadeshield solar control film blinds and Navigation Bridge solar control screens, as well as Digital Image Blinds, have helped make the name of Swift Blinds and Curtains known internationally.

But the name is also one familiar to thousands of local folk. Blinds today are now both a mainstream and fashion product, a long way from the very limited choice back in 1969.

Local shops, local businesses and thousands of local homes have been enhanced by installing beautiful blinds and curtains bearing the Swift name.

Swift blinds can now be found in places as far away as Kuwait, Saudi Arabia, Moscow, Gibraltar, Nigeria, France, Germany and Portugal. And according to rumour they've even been spotted in Venice!

Top: Alan Swift (second right) pictured with sons Nicolas (left) and Christian, and daughter-in-law Caroline, 1994.
Below: Swift Blinds new showroom, 2005.

Dresser Roots - There she blows!

from the 'town gas' before it was sent into the distribution network and was adopted by many gas authorities who were impressed by the smoother running of their services made possible by the improved quality of gas going through their pipes. One gas company reported drops in complaints from 200 per day to just two, and noticed a considerable benefit as far as the cost of routine maintenance was concerned.

At around the same time as the Holmes operation was getting off the ground in Huddersfield two brothers, Philander and Francis Roots, were developing a rotary positive air blower known as the 'Roots Blower' in Connersville, Indiana, USA. In 1927 WC Holmes built these blowers under a licensing agreement, and continued to manufacture its own blower when the agreement expired, gradually improving the design.

From 1973 until 1990 the company traded as Peabody Holmes when it was taken over by Dresser Industries and became parts of its Roots division. The Huddersfield works became the metric plant and the organisation continued to be a leading force in the world-wide blower market.

Dresser Roots, manufacturers of blowers and compressors, based in St Andrews Road Turnbridge, has been an important contributor to the wealth of the Huddersfield area since 1850. It was in that year that WC Holmes & Company Ltd was established at the Turnbridge Works: today the company is part of a giant American conglomerate.

William Cartwright Holmes, founder of the original company, initiated the design and production of the plant for the treatment of gas installations and the recovery and refining of by-products. His innovations included a 'brush' washer which had a dramatically beneficial effect on the purification of coal-generated gas. The company built up an impressive range of gas treatment products, including a revolutionary patented 'dri-gas' plant. This process involved the extraction of water vapour and naphthalene

Above: Founder William Cartwright Holmes.
Right: A Certificate presented to PF Holmes by his father WC Holmes in recognition of sixty years service.

Dresser Industries merged with the Halliburton company in 1998 to form the world's largest provider of products and services to the global petroleum and energy market. At the Huddersfield site the company which became known as DMD-Roots continued to design, manufacture and sell a range of air and gas blowers and vacuum pumps. The main markets

serviced are water and wastewater treatment, bulk handling, process, chemical and petrochemical, pulp and paper as well as general industry.

Halliburton sold all its Dresser companies to two financial institutions in the USA in 2001. The Group became Dresser Inc. Dresser Roots Huddersfield became part of DIUK Ltd.

In 1998 there had been 125 employees (65 shopfloor, 55 staff), seven years later there would be 66 employees (32 shopfloor, 34 staff). European competition had taken some of its market share - lack of investment in infrastructure, manufacturing and new product development had not helped.

The XLP tri-lobe blower had been introduced in 1998. This was to be the last new product introduction until the EasyAir package launched in 2005. A seven year gap in product development resulted in a company not simply standing still but actually going backwards.

Numerous management changes and a lack of stability placed the company in danger of becoming the archetypal old fashioned and outdated British engineering company like Triumph and British Leyland.

Greater stability had been achieved in 2002 under better management. Even so in 2003 the company faced closure. Happily the company's fortunes turned around in 2004 which saw a healthy profit.

Fighting back the company began to regain its former market share. Sales divisions are now established in Shanghai to serve the Asia Pacific market and in Dubai to serve the Middle East and North Africa.

In 2005 sales in China, the home of cheap products and with 81 domestic competitors, would reach £2.3 million. In the Asia Pacific market as a whole sales would be £4.2 million.

A number of new product designs and upgrades are under development. Investment is being made in developing and training new employees, as well as money being spent on buildings and new machinery. The number of employees beginning to rise.

The company has regained pride in itself, and in the fact that Dresser Roots is the manufacturer of the 'original Roots blower' a name known world-wide throughout the industry.

Above: An early section of the Machine Shop.

Queensgate Market -
The Queen of Indoor Market Shopping Centres

What makes a building part of our heritage? How old does it have to be in order to count as something of both interest and importance?

Many folk would say that nothing built since the 1950s has any merit at all. Others may pause to point out that many 'new' buildings have now been around so long that that have not only have been around long enough to become familiar but have also been part of the scene for more than half of most folk's lifetimes. Age of course is not the only criterion by which to judge worth: there's architectural merit too. One such modern building which can now claim both age and merit is the Queensgate Market, a building which in 2005 was being considered for listing by English Heritage after plans were tentatively put forward for its demolition.

Right: A 1950s view of Queensgate's predecessor - the old Market Hall on King Street. Below: Taken soon after opening in 1970 this view from the ring road shows Queensgate's unique roof design and the work of German sculptor Fritz Steller.

The Queensgate Market opened in 1970 replacing the previous market built in 1878. Most of the shops in the old market moved into the new building and the old market closed, before it was demolished soon after.

The most striking feature of the new market was its roof structure based on 21 'asymmetric hyperbolic

paraboloid' shells looking like so many giant mushrooms. The height of the roof shells vary by about three feet or so to allow the greatest possible amount of natural light to reach the stalls. According to its architects, the J Seymour Harris Partnership, the building was the first European example of a vertical patent glazed roof of this type.

Outside, facing the ring road, is a huge modern art ceramic sculpture given the title 'Articulation in Movement'. Made from Stourbridge clay the work was produced and fired between March and October 1969 in a special kiln built for the project, reaching temperatures of up to 1300 centigrade intended to ensure a hardness even greater than that of local stone. The feature is the work of German sculptor Fritz Steller, then working in Stratford-upon-Avon. The sculpture covers some 4,500 square feet and is made up of nine large panels, together with a 32 foot tall sculpture surrounding the Queensgate staircase leading to the market

As the first summer progressed, heat and ventilation problems became all too apparent. The winter which followed revealed unsuitable heating and a leaky roof. But in spite of these faults, a design said to have been built to councillors' demands for a notable building - but cheap to build - the market thrived throughout the seventies and eighties.

The market was the first major building in the town centre to be decorated and have Christmas lights. The money for these was raised by the tenants themselves. Santa has been installed in his grotto there every year since 1975.

On the market's 21st birthday the Queensgate Market Tenants' Association commissioned a huge birthday cake from baker Brian Harrison which was cut up and handed out to customers on the day.

With other new shopping developments through the 1990s in and around the town the Market's drawing power came under strain, the mix of trades changed with the loss of several food shops being replaced mainly by clothing and other niche services stalls.

Now the Market is beginning to improve again. This positive change is continuing largely due to the shopping public's waning appetite for soulless supermarkets and repetitive multiples found in shopping malls. The 75 tenants in the Market today offer a unique service to their customers each being an expert in their own speciality.

Looking forward, who knows? Some have high hopes that the newly listed building will be refurbished and remain forever as an indoor market shopping centre, others would be happy to move to a new site with a new building and more sympathetic to the comfort and convenience expected by today's customers. But whatever the future brings, we can be sure that the hard work, entrepreneurship and customer service for which Queensgate Market Tenant's are famed will ensure that they will continue to trade and flourish somewhere in Huddersfield for generations to come.

Top left: *This coat of arms is located at the Peel Street end of Queensgate Market. It was originally fixed above the entrance to the County Borough of Huddersfield Police Station which was formally on this site, erected in 1898 and demolished 1967.* ***Above:*** *Everything under one roof: one of the many stalls in Queensgate.* ***Below:*** *Queensgate 's Arcade has welcomed generations of shoppers.*

J & E Dickinson - Longley Farm

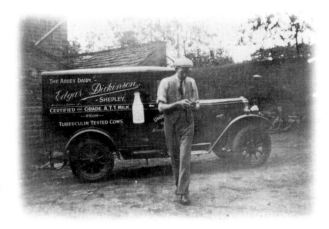

It was a proud moment for Holmfirth's Edgar Dickinson when he was awarded an MBE in 2005. But remarkably he wasn't the first in the family to be honoured by the Queen: in 1990 Edgar's brother Joseph received an OBE.

The brothers are the founders of Longley Farm, an enterprise which today is one of the largest and most well respected privately owned dairies in Britain.

In the 21st century the Longley Farm brand of dairy products is known not just in Huddersfield and Holmfirth but far and wide. Achieving international recognition has been a long story.

The Dickinson brothers came from a farming and dairying background. Their father Edgar Dickinson senior had been a farming contractor based at Field Head Farm in Shepley, and had also run a dairy business, the Abbey Dairy, in the 1920s

and 30s. The brothers however, both became apprentice engineers. During the second world war Edgar worked at Hopkinsons engineering whilst Joseph served in the Navy.

After the war the brothers moved into agricultural contracting themselves, but in 1948 their Great Uncle, Jonas Hinchliffe, of Upper Longley Farm died and bequeathed the farm to them. They got 40 acres, ten cows, a Clydesdale horse - and debts greater than the value of the legacy!

A year later the brothers were able to buy the 30 acre Lower Longley Farm at auction for £2,350.

Their first activities were keeping sheep and poultry, and growing turnips and potatoes, as well as bottling milk. Already highly progressive, the milk was not only free from tuberculosis but also pasteurised.

By 1953 the brothers had moved from hand-milking in a barn to machine-milking in a milking parlour. Milk was sold to Barnsley and Huddersfield Co-ops. They also bought a

*Top: Edgar Dickinson Snr delivering TT milk around Shepley at 4d/pint. **Left** Edgar Dickinson Snr delivering during the big snow of 1932. **Below:** 1960 Joseph & Edgar Dickinson load bottles of cream for delivery. Popular sizes were 1/4pt, 1/3pt and 1/2pt.*

Much of the original farm remains, but it now nestles amongst a highly efficient, ultra modern business, belying its rustic exterior.

Despite the changes however, Longley Farm has remained true to its roots, and both the site and the business have been developed with conservation in mind. The dairy's energy conservation programme has set it apart from others in the industry, not least with its wind turbine generator installed in 1986 standing on the hill overlooking Holmfirth.

By the early 1990s, with frozen cream, Longley Farm had become Britain's largest exporter of frozen food outside the EEC. Development would continue in the late 1990s with the establishment of dairies in Estonia and Australia.

Longley Farm celebrated the millennium by opening its own dairy shop in Holmfirth: 'Longley's'.

separator and began making cream; the first major outlet being a stall on Oldham Market. Selling on doorsteps and through local bakers and confectioners, the business grew.

In 1956 a licence was obtained from the Milk Marketing Board to take in milk from other farms for processing, and the brothers now began to build up a modest daily intake of 200 gallons, selling the produce over a 30-mile wide area.

By the 1960s Longley Farm had become one of the largest private creameries in the country, producing up to 40,000 gallons of cream each month.

Investment continued, and in 1969 a dam was built for cooling water, and back up electrical generators were installed to insure against any future power failures.

Also in 1969 the firm began producing its award winning yoghurt, and now produces sixteen whole milk flavours and six more in its Virtually Fat Free BA range.

In 1972 cottage cheese was being made: the first time it had been made on a large scale anywhere outside the USA.

Tyers Hall Farm in Barnsley was acquired in 1973, a farm which specialised originally in Channel Island milk and later in Jersey milk.

Longley Farm has come a long way since Joseph and Edgar Dickinson inherited their typical Pennine farm; from a small herd of just ten cows milked by hand to the present day internationally-renowned business, now run by Joseph's son, Jimmy.

Today milk is processed using state of the art equipment including reverse osmosis and ultra filtration apparatus, both of which were technological firsts. Dairy production is unrecognisable from the early days when deliveries were made from the back seat of a car - days when no-one ever imagined that the still-future Queen would one day take an interest in what the Dickinsons were up to.

Top left: Vera Jessop filling cream by jug and hand capping the foil lids. Paper cartons were being tried as replacements for glass bottles. ***Below:*** *May 1954 In the yard at Upper Longley Farm, with grey Fergie tractor - from left Kenneth Heeley, Maurice Major, Dennis Charlesworth, Edgar & Joseph Dickinson. Maurice Major worked at Longley Farm for 45 years from 1951 until he retired in 1996.*

Quarmby Promotions

Picture a man in a cloth cap trundling a hand cart round the streets of the West Riding in the 1870s. That was the genesis of the company that today has blue-chip standing and a customer base spanning breweries and airlines, oil companies and multi-nationals.

The man? John Quarmby. The contents of the handcart? Paper bags. Joe set up in Slaithwaite in 1872. His assets were one room doubling as office and warehouse, the cart for deliveries and determination. The last-named quality still motivates Quarmby's today as it uses the latest digital techniques on its ever-widening spectrum of products.

Joe's bags deserved to be successful. He tested heavy-duty ones by filling them with bricks. Soon he took on a boy to make deliveries, in 1889 his elder son became a partner and by 1896, Joe was set up in 'proper' premises in Huddersfield and had bought his first bag-making machines. In 1906 his business became a limited liability company and moved to bigger premises, but on April 15th 1912, the day of the Titanic disaster, the factory was destroyed by fire. Joe rebuilt it. As part of his new start he decided to concentrate on the making of cardboard boxes.

The business continued to diversify, installing in 1931, plant for the manufacture of printed absorbent drip mats, a side line at first but quickly becoming a success.

Now a world leader in printing beer mats, with a board mill and an additional manufacturing site in Germany and a sales office in Belgium. The company supplies a full range of promotional items including ashtrays, clocks, ice buckets, drip trays, waiter trays, bar runners ... the list is endless.

Drip mats have always held a unique place in British culture. They are regarded as a tactile, friendly, non-intrusive advertising medium, appealing to both male and females. With quantities starting from just 5,000 they are a cost effective promotional item.

Pictures: *Interior and exterior views of the Quarmby site.*

Pearson Funeral Services

Pearson Funeral Service, located in Manchester Road Marsden, traces its origins back to the 1920s. It was in 1920 that 23 year old Alfred Bagley established a joinery business and funeral service based in the now demolished Old silk Mill at Warehouse Hill.

Alfred was the son of the Station Master at Marsden; after having trained as master joiner he had originally set up a joiners shop in a converted blacksmiths on Manchester Road.

Alfred's wife, Carrie, did the clerical work looking after the telephone and office. The Bagleys' son, Peter later joined the firm, eventually taking over the business in 1962.

Founder, Alfred Bagley, died in 1982 at the age of 84.

The firm was taken over by Clive Pearson in 2003 when Peter Bagley took semi-retirement.

Clive Pearson trained locally as a funeral director and embalmer from the age of 15.

Clive has other skills too. He recalls arriving at a church for a funeral only to discover that the organist was being driven away in the back of an ambulance. Luckily Clive plays the organ and was able to step into the breach.

Nothing is too much trouble: Clive also recalls an occasion when he and his drivers had to act as waiters and barmen when a hotel booked to provide a funeral tea had forgotten to put the event in their diary.

Today all coffins are bought-in which results in a far larger choice than in the past.

Not much else had changed down the years: until 1957, when the chapel of rest opened, before that the deceased were laid out at home; and hearses and limousines were hired from carriage masters rather than being owned by the firm. Until the 1940s, when a crematorium opened in Manchester, there was no alternative to burial.

Costs too have changed significantly: in the 1930s a burial cost as little as £21; today up to £3,000 is not unusual.

The funeral home was fully renovated in 2005.

Yet though much has changed some things remain unaltered: this family business still provides a careful, caring service, sensitive to its clients needs, 24 hours each day on 365 days a year.

Top left: *Founder Mr Alfred Bagley.*
Left: *Clive Pearson and Peter Bagley.*
Below: *Pearson Funeral Service's premises, 2005.*

Acknowledgments

Morris Bray, who took most of the photographs in this book

Andrew Mitchell

Steve Ainsworth

All reasonable steps were taken by the publishers of this book to trace the copyright holders and obtain permission to use the photographs contained herein. However, due to the passage of time certain individuals were untraceable. Should any interested party subsequently come to light, the publishers can be contacted at the phone number printed at the front of this book and the appropriate arrangements will then be made.

True North Books Ltd - Book List

Memories of Accrington - 1 903204 05 4

Memories of Barnet - 1 903204 16 X

Memories of Barnsley - 1 900463 11 3

More Memories of Barnsley - 1 903 204 79 8

Golden Years of Barnsley -1 900463 87 3

Memories of Basingstoke - 1 903204 26 7

Memories of Bedford - 1 900463 83 0

More Memories of Bedford - 1 903204 33 X

Golden Years of Birmingham - 1 900463 04 0

Birmingham Memories - 1 903204 45 3

More Birmingham Memories - 1 903204 80 1

Memories of Blackburn - 1 900463 40 7

More Memories of Blackburn - 1 900463 96 2

Memories of Blackpool - 1 900463 21 0

Memories of Bolton - 1 900463 45 8

More Memories of Bolton - 1 900463 13 X

Bolton Memories - 1 903204 37 2

Memories of Bournemouth -1 900463 44 X

Memories of Bradford - 1 900463 00 8

More Memories of Bradford - 1 900463 16 4

More Memories of Bradford II - 1 900463 63 6

Bradford Memories - 1 903204 47 X

Bradford City Memories - 1 900463 57 1

Memories of Bristol - 1 900463 78 4

More Memories of Bristol - 1 903204 43 7

Memories of Bromley - 1 903204 21 6

Memories of Burnley - 1 900463 95 4

Golden Years of Burnley - 1 900463 67 9

Memories of Bury - 1 900463 90 3

More Memories of Bury - 1 903 204 78 X

Memories of Cambridge - 1 900463 88 1

Memories of Cardiff - 1 900463 14 8

More Memories of Cardiff - 1 903204 73 9

Memories of Carlisle - 1 900463 38 5

Memories of Chelmsford - 1 903204 29 1

Memories of Cheltenham - 1 903204 17 8

Memories of Chester - 1 900463 46 6

More Memories of Chester -1 903204 02 X

Chester Memories - 1 903204 83 6

Memories of Chesterfield -1 900463 61 X

More Memories of Chesterfield - 1 903204 28 3

Memories of Colchester - 1 900463 74 1

Nostalgic Coventry - 1 900463 58 X

Coventry Memories - 1 903204 38 0

Memories of Croydon - 1 900463 19 9

More Memories of Croydon - 1 903204 35 6

Golden Years of Darlington - 1 900463 72 5

Nostalgic Darlington - 1 900463 31 8

Darlington Memories - 1 903204 46 1

Memories of Derby - 1 900463 37 7

More Memories of Derby - 1 903204 20 8

Memories of Dewsbury & Batley - 1 900463 80 6

Memories of Doncaster - 1 900463 36 9

More Memories of Doncaster - 1 903204 75 5

Nostalgic Dudley - 1 900463 03 2

Golden Years of Dudley - 1 903204 60 7

Memories of Edinburgh - 1 900463 33 4

More memories of Edinburgh - 1903204 72 0

Memories of Enfield - 1 903204 14 3

Memories of Exeter - 1 900463 94 6

Memories of Glasgow - 1 900463 68 7

More Memories of Glasgow - 1 903204 44 5

Memories of Gloucester - 1 903204 04 6

Memories of Grimsby - 1 900463 97 0

More Memories of Grimsby - 1 903204 36 4

Memories of Guildford - 1 903204 22 4

Memories of Halifax - 1 900463 05 9

More Memories of Halifax - 1 900463 06 7

Golden Years of Halifax - 1 900463 62 8

Nostalgic Halifax - 1 903204 30 5

Memories of Harrogate - 1 903204 01 1

Memories of Hartlepool - 1 900463 42 3

Memories of High Wycombe - 1 900463 84 9

Memories of Huddersfield - 1 900463 15 6

More Memories of Huddersfield - 1 900463 26 1

Golden Years of Huddersfield - 1 900463 77 6

Nostalgic Huddersfield - 1 903204 19 4

Huddersfield Memories - 1903204 86 0

Huddersfield Town FC - 1 900463 51 2

Memories of Hull - 1 900463 86 5

More Memories of Hull - 1 903204 06 2

Hull Memories - 1 903204 70 4

True North Books Ltd - Book List

Memories of Keighley - 1 900463 01 6

Golden Years of Keighley - 1 900463 92 X

Memories of Kingston - 1 903204 24 0

Memories of Leeds - 1 900463 75 X

More Memories of Leeds - 1 900463 12 1

Golden Years of Leeds - 1 903204 07 0

Memories of Leicester - 1 900463 08 3

Leeds Memories - 1 903204 62 3

More Memories of Leicester - 1 903204 08 9

Memories of Leigh - 1 903204 27 5

Memories of Lincoln - 1 900463 43 1

Memories of Liverpool - 1 900463 07 5

More Memories of Liverpool - 1 903204 09 7

Liverpool Memories - 1 903204 53 4

Memories of Luton - 1 900463 93 8

Memories of Macclesfield - 1 900463 28 8

Memories of Manchester - 1 900463 27 X

More Memories of Manchester - 1 903204 03 8

Manchester Memories - 1 903204 54 2

Memories of Middlesbrough - 1 900463 56 3

More Memories of Middlesbrough - 1 903204 42 9

Memories of Newbury - 1 900463 79 2

Memories of Newcastle - 1 900463 81 4

More Memories of Newcastle - 1 903204 10 0

Newcastle Memories - 1.903204 71 2

Memories of Newport - 1 900463 59 8

Memories of Northampton - 1 900463 48 2

More Memories of Northampton - 1 903204 34 8

Memories of Norwich - 1 900463 73 3

Memories of Nottingham - 1 900463 91 1

More Memories of Nottingham - 1 903204 11 9

Nottingham Memories - 1 903204 63 1

Bygone Oldham - 1 900463 25 3

Memories of Oldham - 1 900463 76 8

More Memories of Oldham - 1 903204 84 4

Memories of Oxford - 1 900463 54 7

Memories of Peterborough - 1 900463 98 9

Golden Years of Poole - 1 900463 69 5

Memories of Portsmouth - 1 900463 39 3

More Memories of Portsmouth - 1 903204 51 8

Nostalgic Preston - 1 900463 50 4

More Memories of Preston - 1 900463 17 2

Preston Memories - 1 903204 41 0

Memories of Reading - 1 900463 49 0

Memories of Rochdale - 1 900463 60 1

More Memories of Reading - 1 903204 39 9

More Memories of Rochdale - 1 900463 22 9

Memories of Romford - 1 903204 40 2

Memories of Rothertham- 1903204 77 1

Memories of St Albans - 1 903204 23 2

Memories of St Helens - 1 900463 52 0

Memories of Sheffield - 1 900463 20 2

More Memories of Sheffield - 1 900463 32 6

Golden Years of Sheffield - 1 903204 13 5

Memories of Slough - 1 900 463 29 6

Golden Years of Solihull - 1 903204 55 0

Memories of Southampton - 1 900463 34 2

More Memories of Southampton - 1 903204 49 6

Memories of Stockport - 1 900463 55 5

More Memories of Stockport - 1 903204 18 6

Memories of Stockton - 1 900463 41 5

Memories of Stoke-on-Trent - 1 900463 47 4

More Memories of Stoke-on-Trent - 1 903204 12 7

Memories of Stourbridge - 1903204 31 3

Memories of Sunderland - 1 900463 71 7

More Memories of Sunderland - 1 903204 48 8

Memories of Swindon - 1 903204 00 3

Memories of Uxbridge - 1 900463 64 4

Memories of Wakefield - 1 900463 65 2

More Memories of Wakefield - 1 900463 89 X

Nostalgic Walsall - 1 900463 18 0

Golden Years of Walsall - 1 903204 56 9

More Memories of Warrington - 1 900463 02 4

Warrington Memories - 1 903204 85 2

Memories of Watford - 1 900463 24 5

Golden Years of West Bromwich - 1 900463 99 7

Memories of Wigan - 1 900463 85 7

Golden Years of Wigan - 1 900463 82 2

More Memories of Wigan - 1 903204 82 8

Nostalgic Wirral - 1 903204 15 1

Wirral Memories - 1 903204 747

Memories of Woking - 1 903204 32 1

Nostalgic Wolverhampton - 1 900463 53 9

Wolverhampton Memories - 1 903204 50 X

Memories of Worcester - 1 903204 25 9

Memories of Wrexham - 1 900463 23 7

Memories of York - 1 900463 66 0